The Home Pro Bathroom and Kitchen Remodeling Guide

HOW TO USE THIS BOOK

For any of the jobs in this book, you'll find detailed step-by-step instructions. The steps are completely illustrated to show exactly what is meant by the instruction.

Before beginning any job, it is a good idea to first read through the entire procedure. You will be told the equipment, tools and supplies you need. Also, you will get a pretty good idea of just what skills and time are involved.

Once you begin the job, proceed step-by-step. Be sure to read any information in front of the step. Because the step is keyed directly to the illustration, learn to refer to the illustration while you are reading. It may be slower reading but it's faster understanding.

You will find Home Pro tips throughout the book. Often, the Home Pro is pointing out a shortcut or a tip which will make the job easier. At other times, he is giving you information which the novice is likely to overlook. Read what he tells you — you can be a Home Pro yourself.

BATHROOM REMODELING

KITCHEN REMODELING

BATHROOM REMODELING

BATHROOM REMODELING

Bathroom remodeling has become a relatively common family project. New materials and fixtures are available which can add greatly to the appearance of older bathrooms. In addition, many of the new bathroom items on the market, in particular the prefabricated structures, are produced with an eye to the growing "do-it-yourself" trend and simplify the remodeling task considerably.

In making your remodeling plans, you will probably not be examining a single bathroom in isolation. In place of the former all-purpose family bathroom, the trend has been to multiple bathrooms. Often, each bathroom has a different function; e.g. master bathroom, children's bathroom, half bath or powder room, etc. Thus, you must determine the intended use of the bathroom. Decisions that we will be discussing later, such as choice of fixtures, will depend on the intended use of the bathroom.

Remodeling covers a wide range of activities such as simple redecorating with a coat of paint and new curtains, major installation of new fixtures and new wall, floor and ceiling coverings. You may find that your needs will be satisfied with nothing less than the addition of a new bathroom. While we do not specifically discuss adding a bathroom, much of the information provided will be useful to you in adding a bathroom.

To help in your planning, you should also take stock of how old your children are now and what their future needs will be. As children become teenagers, they usually place much greater demand on existing bathroom facilities. Also, do you expect your family to grow, either with the addition of more children or from grandparents who move in? Any special requirements like these should be accounted for in your planning now.

We will now consider more specifically the features of a good bathroom. With this as background, we will then be better able to discuss selection of fixtures and other bathroom equipment. Knowledge of the new products available will help you plan an attractive, functional bathroom for your family's enjoyment.

BEFORE

AFTER

3

FEATURES OF A GOOD BATHROOM

The bathroom has unique requirements setting it off from other rooms in the house. Foremost is the problem of moisture. All surfaces and fixtures must be able to withstand large amounts of moisture, both from condensation and from direct splashing from the wash basin, bathtub and shower. Walls, floor and ceiling materials should be impervious to moisture. Adequate ventilation should be provided to help cope with the moisture problem.

Local heating is usually needed in the bathroom, separate from the central heating of the house. The bathroom is ordinarily small enough to heat quickly and easily, and may be used when the main heating is not in use. Often venting and heat are combined in a single heater-fan unit.

Because of the bathroom's generally restricted size, proper use of the available space becomes quite important. Minimum distances between fixtures have been prescribed for general use and are shown here. However, if you have an infant in the family, you will need more room for maneuvering. Also, if one of the family uses a

4

FEATURES OF A GOOD BATHROOM

wheelchair, the door must be wide enough to accommodate the wheelchair and space must be provided inside the bathroom.

Storage space is at a premium in the bathroom. The well-planned bathroom has space for at least those items which are needed on a day-to-day basis, such as towels, soap, tissue paper, etc.

The bathroom should have adequate facilities to handle peak loads. These will usually occur in the morning, when the family is getting ready for work and school. If the problem becomes acute, another bathroom may be required. But before that point is reached, a double wash basin or compartmentalized fixture can be of help.

GRAB BARS

5

SELECTING FIXTURES

There are many new materials and colors, with different shapes and sizes, available now for bathroom fixtures. The advent of the fiberglass-reinforced plastic line of fixtures, in particular, allows greater flexibility in bathroom planning and design. Large units, even complete bathrooms, can be purchased and assembled in place with little difficulty, provided the basic plumbing and electrical wiring are in.

We will consider, in turn, the major bathroom fixtures: bathtubs/showers, sinks/vanities and toilets.

Bathtub/Showers

The standard bathtub is five feet long, 16 inches high and 30-32 inches wide. Many existing bathrooms were built to a five feet by eight feet size to fit this bathtub. There are now many different sizes and shapes, including square, corner, round, sunken, raised, etc. The material for bathtubs is porcelain-enameled cast iron or pressed steel, or the newer molded, fiberglass-reinforced plastic.

SELECTING FIXTURES

Bathtubs/Showers

In the standard bathtub, the drain and faucets are located at the foot of the tub. Certain models have these in different locations for convenience.

Bathtubs with slip-resistant surfaces are on the market. They are easy to clean and have decorative patterns. Non-skid strips can be bought separately, wavy or straight, in different colors.

The shower is often integral with the bathtub, in which case a shower curtain, sliding glass doors or a folding panel is generally installed over the tub. Glass doors can be decorative or have a mirror finish. The glass should be of the unbreakable, shatterproof type. Curtains allow a periodic change of color scheme and make it easier to clean the bathtub, but permit more leakage than do sliding doors.

Prefabricated bathtub/shower units are available, which include the three surrounding walls in fiberglass-reinforced plastic and all accessories and fittings. In some cases, the walls seal together and to the top of the tub. In other cases, the whole unit may be of one-piece construction.

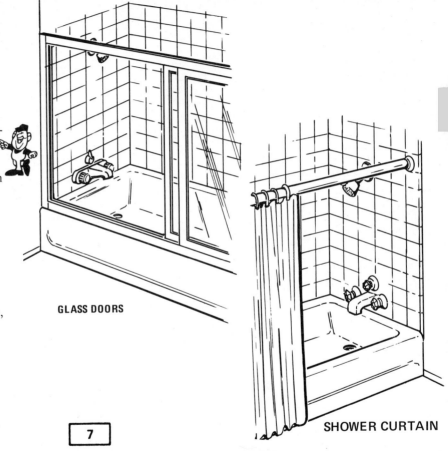

GLASS DOORS

SHOWER CURTAIN

SELECTING FIXTURES

Bathtubs/Showers

When the tub and shower are combined, a
fitting is often used which diverts water from
the tub faucets to the shower head. Or, separate
faucets or a mixer valve may be used. The mixer
valve makes it easy to find the right temperature.
For low water pressure installations, an automatic
temperature control can be installed. This prevents scalding hot water when the cold water is
used in another part of the house. For bathtubs,
there is even a device for automatically setting
temperatures and water level. You can set it and
walk away.

Separate stall showers are now also available as
prefabricated units. These are of porcelain-
enameled steel and fiberglass, and range in floor
size from 30 inches by 30 inches to 36 by 36 to
34 by 48. If desired, the fiberglass units can have
towel racks, soap dishes and seats molded into
the structure.

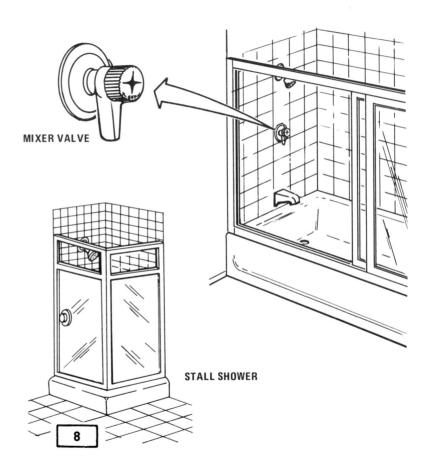

MIXER VALVE

STALL SHOWER

8

SELECTING FIXTURES

Bathtubs/Showers

Whether the shower is integral with the bathtub
or a separate stall, a grab bar should be provided
at a height of about four feet. The shower head
should be installed a few inches above the tallest
user to prevent bumping the head.

The shower head is usually chrome-plated brass,
with a swivel joint to allow directing the spray.
There is a type of shower head which you can
hold in your hand and which is attached to a
flexible metal tube. This is easy to install, since
it can be connected to the tub faucet.

Another type of shower unit has two shower
heads at different heights. They can be used
either separately or together.

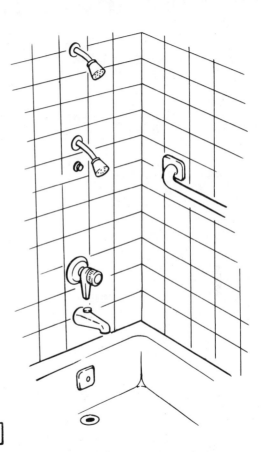

9

SELECTING FIXTURES

Sinks/Vanities

In many older bathrooms, the wash basin has no convenient place for setting things. Moreover, unsightly plumbing under the basin detracts from the appearance of the bathroom. The modern vanity solves both of these problems. It also helps solve a storage space problem, by providing convenient drawers and shelves where they are most needed.

Ready-made vanities are available in many sizes. Typical widths range from 20 inches to 50 inches, and the standard height is 34 inches. A large vanity will be found useful for taking care of the baby. A useful feature for small children is a bottom drawer which is reversible. The children can pull this out and stand on it to reach the wash basin.

Cabinets have different patterns and colors and have single or dual basins. The basins may be rectangular, oval or circular and have different colors. Basins are made of vitreous china, enameled cast iron, porcelain-enameled steel or stainless steel.

SELECTING FIXTURES

Sinks/Vanities

For the color of the basin, you may wish to choose an accent color that goes well with the rest of the bathroom. Dark colors tend to show powder, soap, etc. more easily than lighter colors.

Faucets and fittings are available in chrome finish, white china, or clear acrylic. Separate hot and cold water faucets are most common, but single action levers are also available. Most basins have pop-up drains, with an overflow opening in front.

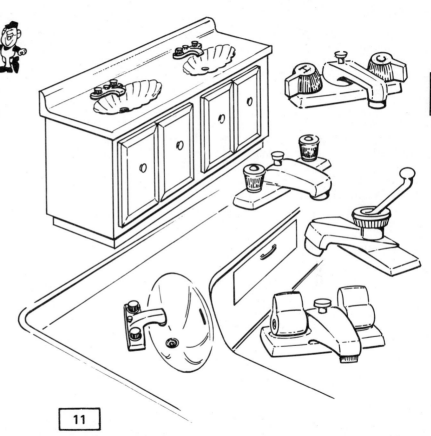

SELECTING FIXTURES

Toilets

Most toilets are free-standing, but wall-hung models have been on the market for some time. These models are more expensive, but make it easier to clean around the toilet.

According to their action, toilets are classed as wash down, reverse trap or siphon jets, or siphon vortex. The washdown is the least expensive and also the noisiest. The trapway is at the front of the bowl and the water surface is small.

The reverse trap and siphon jet have the trapway at the rear of the bowl. They are similar, but the siphon jet has a larger trapway and water surface, is quieter, and is more expensive.

The best and most expensive fixture is the siphon vortex, an improvement on the siphon jet.

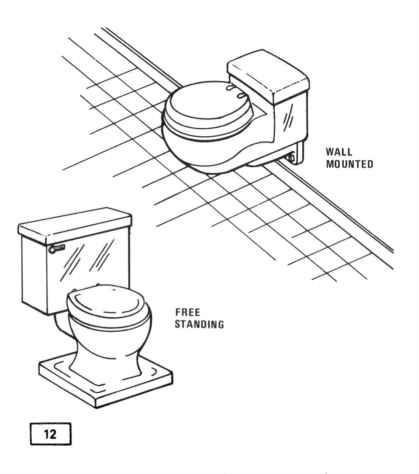

WALL MOUNTED

FREE STANDING

12

SELECTING FIXTURES

Toilets

Any of the different types of toilets can be used with a flush valve instead of a water tank. If there is sufficient water pressure, the flush valve can be used to eliminate the wait that is necessary between flushings with a water tank. However, the flush valve uses more water.

Instead of the high tank, models are available with a low tank only slightly higher than the toilet seat. These are one-piece, free-standing units. Toilets are also available with tanks shaped to fit in a corner.

Toilets can also be obtained with a silent flush. These models are more expensive, but the location may make such a feature desirable.

The most common material is vitreous china, with enameled cast iron also used. Units are available in different colors, and the covers are sometimes treated as decorator items.

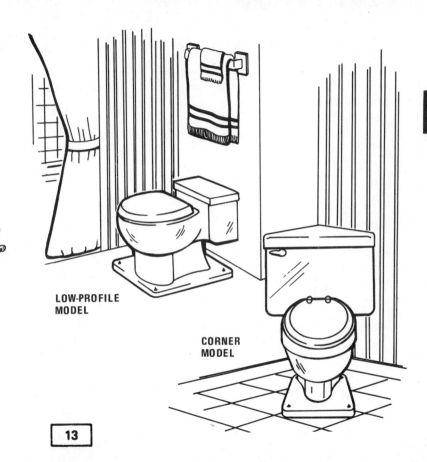

LOW-PROFILE MODEL

CORNER MODEL

LIGHTING, HEATING AND VENTILATION

Lighting

Good lighting is needed in the bathroom for shaving, cosmetic application, manicuring and other personal grooming operations. It is also needed for reading labels, if medicines are stored in the bathroom.

For minimum-size bathrooms, lighting over the sink/vanity is probably sufficient for the entire room. Most bathrooms, however, should have general lighting in addition to the lighting at the vanity.

Lighting at the sink/vanity should be arranged to illuminate the face of the user as he or she looks into the mirror. Glare and shadows should be avoided by using diffuse light. Wall features on each side and top of the mirror will serve the purpose. If fluorescent tubes are used, the White Warm Deluxe (WWX) type is more flattering to the complexion than the cool variety.

A soffit light over the vanity also works well, as an alternative.

14

LIGHTING, HEATING AND VENTILATION

Lighting

General lighting can be provided by several fluorescent lights in the ceiling. If the ceiling is high, a suspended ceiling can be used with covered fluorescent lights. A luminous ceiling can now be purchased as a package unit.

General illumination is aided by light-colored walls, ceiling and vanity top. Mirrors also increase the general level of illumination, and increase the apparent size of a bathroom.

Any light fixtures over the shower or bathtub should be watertight and vapor proof.

Other kinds of lights now on the market which often are used in the bathroom include heat lamps, sun lamps and ozone lamps.

These are for heat, suntans and air freshening, respectively. However, wiring codes should be checked before installing these lamps.

For bathrooms with insufficient natural light from windows, a skylight can be a solution. The skylight will also improve ventilation.

15

LIGHTING, HEATING AND VENTILATION

Heating

The bathroom is relatively easy to heat and should have heating separate from the main house system. A variety of heaters is available for this purpose, both electric and gas.

The heater is sometimes combined with lighting, as with a heat lamp, or with ventilation in an exhaust blower/heater unit.

A heater, such as the common flush-mounted, wall type, should not be installed too close to the toilet or it will be uncomfortable. Portable heaters should not be used in the bathroom, for safety reasons. Any electric heater should be properly grounded. Gas heaters must be vented.

Ventilation

If there is no window, a ventilation fan may be required by code. Even if there is a window, it is often advisable to install a fan to help evacuate moisture and odors.

Many self-contained wall or ceiling-mounted ventilation units are available on the market.

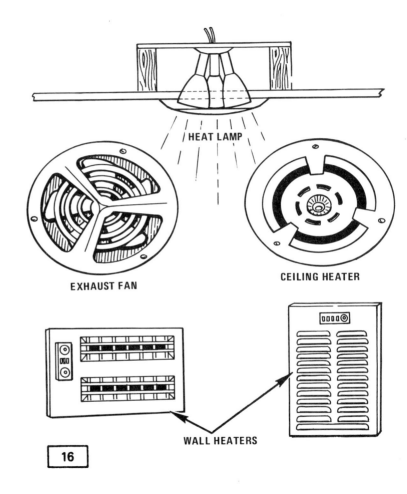

HEAT LAMP

EXHAUST FAN

CEILING HEATER

WALL HEATERS

16

CABINETS AND ACCESSORIES

Many bathrooms suffer from insufficient storage space. This is partly due to their small size, but can also be attributed to improper use of existing space. Storage can be increased by using modern cabinets designed to hang on the wall or fit between studs, by using towel ladders or pole shelves and by means of a vanity, utilizing the space beneath the wash basin.

Another possibility is to use the space behind and above the toilet. If the toilet is moved forward about a foot, there is room for a floor-to-ceiling built-in wall cabinet. Or a pole with shelves can perhaps be installed without moving the toilet.

It is common to find a medicine cabinet with a mirror front over the wash basin. A typical cabinet fits into a 16 x 22 inch opening between the studs, with an overall size of 28 inches wide by 32 inches high. Other sizes are also available. These cabinets have adjustable shelves of glass, plastic or metal. The distance from the floor to the bottom of the cabinet should be 4 to 4-1/2 feet.

17

CABINETS AND ACCESSORIES

Other cabinets similar to the medicine cabinet can be installed elsewhere in the bathroom for cleaning supplies, linens, etc. These cabinets are typically eight to ten inches deep but project only four to six inches, since they fit between the studs.

Convenient storage is needed for the increasing variety of electrical bathroom appliances, such as hair dryers, electric shavers, etc. A sufficient number of electrical outlets should be provided for these items. These outlets should be near the mirror, should be grounded and should not be affected by the light switch. They should remain "live" whether the lights are on or off. The light switches, for added safety, should be located where they cannot be reached by a person using the bathtub, shower or wash basin.

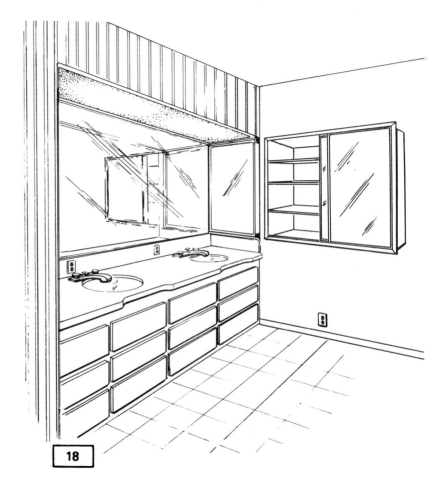

18

CABINETS AND ACCESSORIES

Accessories for the bathroom include a wide variety of towel bars and racks, toothbrush holders, paper holders, soap dishes, etc. These are available in different materials and finishes including vinyl, polished or brushed brass or chrome, and aluminum. Some items such as towel rods and soap dishes, are also available in glass. For safety, these should not be used.

More recent accessories include lotion and soap dispensers, retractable clothes line, concealed scales, magazine rack and others. A clothes hamper is often a convenience in the bathroom.

Grab bars are a valuable addition to any area that may be slippery, such as bathtub or shower. Different sizes and shapes are available.

A liberal use of mirrors will add a feeling of spaciousness to a bathroom and improve lighting. A full length mirror can be installed on the bathroom door, but should be fastened securely. Other possible locations are on the bathtub sliding door, or on the wall, perhaps concealing a storage area.

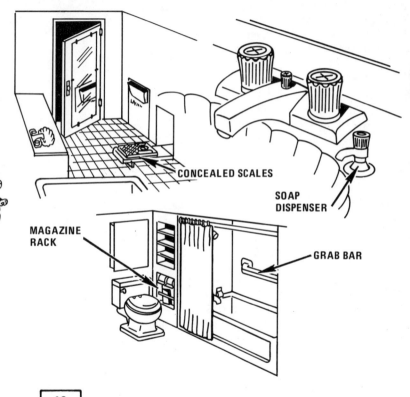

CONCEALED SCALES

SOAP DISPENSER

MAGAZINE RACK

GRAB BAR

19

WALLS, FLOOR AND CEILING

Using the right materials for walls, floor and
ceiling, and installing them properly, will provide
a good foundation for a sound and attractive
bathroom. There is now a very wide variety of
materials that are designed for bathroom use.

Wall Coverings

Some of the standard materials to consider for
wall covering are paint, wallpaper, plastic
laminates, ceramic tile, plastic tile, and plastic-
coated hardboard.

If paint is used, it should be a gloss or semi-gloss
enamel. It should not be used around the bathtub or shower, as it will not stand up.

Many colorful, washable wallpapers are available,
which should be applied with waterproof
adhesive.

Plastic laminate, the material often used on
kitchen countertops, is good for bathroom walls
because it is unaffected by moisture, is extremely
durable and is easily wiped clean. It is particularly appropriate around the bathtub and
shower. Many patterns and colors are available.

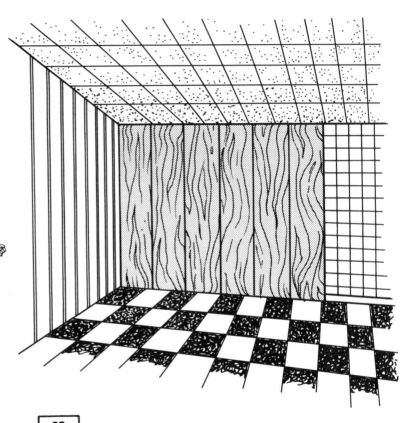

WALLS, FLOOR AND CEILING

Wall Coverings

Ceramic tile is one of the most common and most durable wall coverings. It is often used around bathtubs and showers. If used in this manner, it should extend all the way to the ceiling.

Plastic tile and plastic-coated hardboards are less expensive alternatives which are available in many colors and easy to install.

Other materials are also used on bathroom walls. Mirrors or mirror tiles are sometimes used to cover an entire wall or a large portion thereof. Coated fabrics are colorful and easy to install.

Sheet vinyl is normally found on floors, but, with moisture-resistant backing, it also makes a good bathroom wall covering.

Wall color should be light enough to provide good light reflectance. Strong accent colors are not unusual in the bathroom. To make the room seem larger, the doors and trim should be the same color as the walls.

21

WALLS, FLOOR AND CEILING

Floor Coverings

The bathroom floor covering requires particular attention because of the continuous moisture and high traffic.

Standard materials include ceramic tile, sheet vinyl, vinyl tile, vinyl asbestos tile, and rubber tile. Carpeting is also growing in popularity.

Ceramic tile provides an extremely durable, impervious surface if installed properly. It is cold and hard.

Sheet vinyl gives a seamless surface. There is a wide choice of colors, patterns and textures. Vinyl tile and the other tiles are easier to install, but have the disadvantage of producing seams where moisture can collect and perhaps penetrate.

Carpeting has clear advantages and disadvantages. It is quiet, warm, safe and dropped objects usually do not break. On the other hand, it may wrinkle and bunch up, especially near the door. Children aggravate this problem. If carpeting is used, the underlying floor should be sound, since moisture will soak through the carpet.

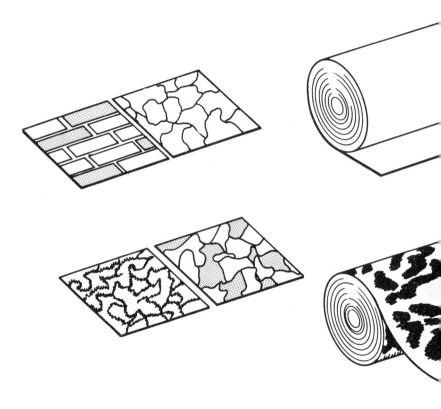

WALLS, FLOOR AND CEILING

Ceiling

Standard ceiling materials include lath and plaster, gypsum board or wall board, tile or panels for a suspended ceiling. Lath and plaster should be installed by a professional. Wallboard, tile and suspended ceilings can be handled by the homeowner.

Tiles are available in a variety of colors, patterns and textures. They can be attached either directly to the existing ceiling, using adhesive, or to furring strips using staples or nails. The sizes of tiles are commonly 12 inches by 12 inches or 12 inches by 24 inches.

Panels are used to construct suspended ceilings. They are designed to slip into place in a framework or grid which is suspended from an existing ceiling. Sizes are 24 inches by 24 inches and 24 inches by 48 inches.

Suspended ceilings are used to hide unsightly pipes or wires and are used with translucent panels to provide luminous ceilings.

23

HOW TO PROCEED

Making Your Plan

Before doing any remodeling or having it done by someone else, you should make a scale drawing of your bathroom. A good scale to use is 1/2 inch equals one foot. This will help you visualize where everything is going to be and whether it will fit properly. You can cut out scale-sized templates and try different arrangements. Once you have arrived at a suitable plan, it can serve as a guide to both you and your contractors.

Accurate measurement is particularly important in the bathroom, where space is restricted. In making your measurements, you need to consider more than just whether a fixture, such as a bathtub or vanity, will fit in the available space. You should, in addition, check that

- the hallway, doors, etc., will allow passage of any items to be installed,
- there is sufficient room to work in doing the actual installation.

In arriving at a final plan, review the features of a good bathroom discussed earlier. Be sure the bathroom will serve its intended function and that you have given storage space, lighting, safety and particularly moisture due respect in your plans.

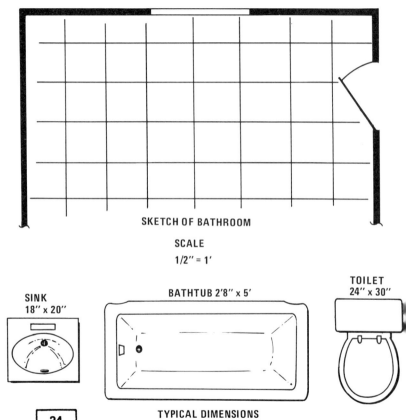

SKETCH OF BATHROOM

SCALE
1/2" = 1'

SINK
18" x 20"

BATHTUB 2'8" x 5'

TOILET
24" x 30"

24

TYPICAL DIMENSIONS

HOW TO PROCEED

Deciding What To Do Yourself

The first step is to learn what things you legally can do yourself. Once you have determined this, then you can decide, from among the tasks legally allowed, what you would like to attempt to do yourself.

Check with your local Department of Building and Safety to see what rules, codes and ordinances apply. These laws vary considerably from one community to another in different parts of the country. It is not necessary to check if you merely plan a new coat of paint, of course, but if you intend any structural changes, plumbing, or electrical work, investigate first. Often a licensed electrician is required for electrical work, and if you deviate, you could invalidate your home fire insurance.

When deciding what to do yourself, bear in mind that dismantling the bathroom, depending on how many bathrooms you have, may affect the entire family. If you have only one bathroom, which is to be remodeled, you might decide to plan a short family vacation. The amount of time that you must go without will usually be less if you have expert help. The expert is also less likely to make costly mistakes, and even if he does, that is his responsibility.

If you're considering a major remodeling job, the best plan is probably a combined effort, where you do the initial preparatory work and the finishing, and you hire expert assistance for the major tasks. You can get the bathroom ready by emptying all the cabinets and removing all decorative items such as curtains, etc. If the cabinets and fixtures are to be removed, you may decide to remove them yourself. Now the professional makes any major structural changes to windows, doors or walls and does the plumbing and electrical work. Whether you should install the fixtures and cabinets or have it done depends on your facility with this kind of work.

Later sections in this book describe how to do these things. Much or perhaps all of the finish work you can do yourself. This may include painting, wallpapering, paneling or laying a new floor. If you are covering the floor in vinyl or carpet, remember that it is easier laying these materials in the tile form than in sheets.

It is essential that you obtain cost estimates before hiring expert help. This is part of the process of selecting contractors.

HOW TO PROCEED

Selecting a Contractor

If you are going to need expert assistance, you should take your plans to several contractors for bids. They may also have suggestions worth listening to. Friends may supply you with names of contractors from past experience. If not, the Yellow Pages are a good source.

Get at least two bids for the proposed work. A bid is a written description of the job including a complete list of work to be done, detailed specifications of materials, equipment manufacture and model number, and itemized costs. The bids should also specify who will obtain the necessary permit(s), if any, and who will do the preparation and cleanup work. It also must be clearly specified who will install what items.

If the two bids are close together in price, choose one of them based on your best judgment. If the bids are, say, 20% or more different, you should get a third bid to ascertain which bid is out of line.

Before making a final contractor selection, it is well to ask for references. These previous customers can tell you if they were satisfied with the contractor's work.

The final agreement, whether it be the bid form or a separate form, should include a schedule of payment, and an arbitration clause. The clause is to protect both parties in case of disagreements that may arise while the work is in progress.

HOW TO PROCEED

Sequence and Schedule

When you have selected your contractor(s), you will, with his help, establish a mutually agreeable schedule. The guiding sequence should be as follows:

- Empty all cabinets and clear bathroom
- Remove old cabinets and fixtures
- Remove flooring and old wall tiles, paper, or paneling
- Make structural alterations in doors, windows, walls
- Repair walls where necessary
- Install subflooring
- Rough-in plumbing connections
- Install new electrical outlets and switches
- Install new fixtures and cabinets
- Remove debris and clean up
- Paint, wallpaper, install new floor
- Add accessories and decorator touches — towel racks, grab bars, curtains, etc.

Inspectors will be required after structural, plumbing and electrical work.

Not all of the above steps may apply to your remodeling job, of course. Just use the list as a guide where it applies. Also, you may want to do some of the tasks more gradually, to keep a portion of the bathroom in use for as long as possible.

REMODELING PROCEDURES

The following pages provide specific procedures for performing those bathroom remodeling activities that you have decided to do yourself. Reading through the procedures may in fact help you in deciding what to attempt yourself. In any case, before starting any of the major jobs, such as REPLACING TOILETS, INSTALLING SHOWERS, etc., read through the procedures. You will find the following hints useful as you read:

- Each page consists of instructions accompanied by illustrations in which items are numbered. These numbers correspond to the numbers in brackets in the instructions. This allows you to easily locate and identify each item.

- The steps are arranged in numbered sequence. This sequence is logical and efficient and should be followed, except in those instances where the instructions route you out of the sequence.

- The procedures are divided into sections by major activity as shown in the contents. For example, the first section is INSTALLING CABINETS. Each section is further divided if necessary, for example, Vanity Cabinets and Wall Cabinets.

- Where there is the possibility of personal injury or damage to equipment, a clear indication of this appears: WARNING if there is a possibility of personal injury, or CAUTION if there is a possibility of equipment damage.

Before starting the specific procedures, certain comments should be made that apply generally to all of the procedures.

1. Manufacturer's Instructions: There is a wide variety of appliances, cabinets, etc. available on the market. Specific instructions for each model cannot conceivably be provided in a book of this scope. Therefore, instructions are presented for typical installations, which should enable you to perform the required tasks. However, it must be emphasized that you should refer to the manufacturer's instructions for your particular model. These will give you important details that cannot be included in the book.

2. Carton Contents: When you order a new appliance, fixture or cabinet, do not remove the old one until you have examined the new one carefully. If you receive a new lavatory in a carton, for example, open the carton, examine the lavatory for defects, and account for all parts. Be sure it is the

REMODELING PROCEDURES

model and size you ordered. Only when satisfied on these counts should you remove the old lavatory.

3. Electrical/Plumbing/Structural Changes: Follow the advice in the preceding planning sections in having contractors perform major changes in electrical wiring, plumbing, or structure of the house. All of the procedures following assume that this basic work has already been accomplished.

4. Methods of Attachment: Most cabinet installations require attachments to walls or ceilings. The attachment should be made to wall studs [2] or ceiling joists [1] where possible. These may be found by using a magnetic stud finder, by rapping on the wall, or by drilling small holes near the edge of the ceiling or near the base board.

For standard attachments to studs or joists, use number 10 wood screws [3]. Screws should be lubricated with soap or wax to make installation easier. Any bumps on the wall should be sandpapered smooth before attachment.

If the studs or joists are not in the proper position for attachment, which is often the case, alternative methods must be used. Three methods are shown here.

For wallboard or lath and plaster use toggle bolts [4] or molly screws [5].

For a masonry surface such as brick or tile, use expanding anchors [6].

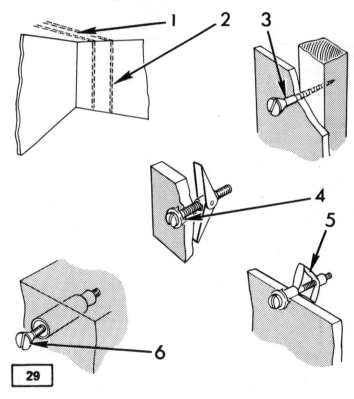

29

INSTALLING CABINETS

Wall Cabinets

Bathroom wall cabinets typically are available as individual units with doors, shelves and essential hardware already installed.

The main concern of the cabinet installer is to get the cabinet mounted level, especially where the wall may not be exactly straight up and down or where the surface may not be even.

Before starting on wall cabinet installation, be sure the following things are done:

- A detailed plan has been prepared specifying the location of each cabinet to be installed.

- All obstacles have been removed from the wall cabinet work area, including the old cabinet.

- Bathtub work is complete.

Wall cabinet installation requires the following tools and supplies:

    Magnetic stud finder
    Pencil
    Spirit level
    Stepladder
    Power drill and 1/8-inch bit
    Common screwdriver
    Claw hammer
    Nails
    Wood shingles or shims
    Wood screws

The above list excludes the cabinet and all supplies normally furnished with the cabinet.

INSTALLING CABINETS

Wall Cabinets

1. If possible, remove shelves from cabinet, to provide better access to mounting rail [2].

2. Locate and mark at least two wall studs [1] at desired cabinet location.

3. Mark wall between studs to indicate desired cabinet height.

4. Have someone else hold cabinet against wall as level as possible in desired location.

5. Fasten cabinet to wall with two nails [3] driven only part way in.

6. Check with level [4] and adjust cabinet position until even, left-to-right.

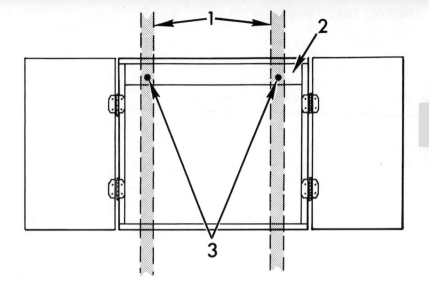

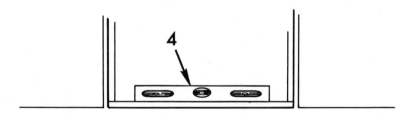

31

INSTALLING CABINETS

Wall Cabinets

7. Adjust cabinet position with plumb and level, using shims as necessary.

8. Secure cabinet to wall with screws [3] through mounting rail [2] into wall studs [1].

9. Remove nails and fill nail holes.

10. Re-install shelves.

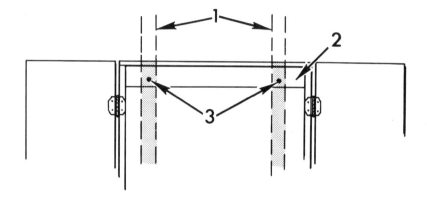

INSTALLING CABINETS

Vanities

Before starting on vanity installation, be sure the following things are done:

- A detailed plan has been prepared, specifying the location and dimensions of the vanity to be installed.

- Bathtub work is complete.

- All obstacles have been removed from the vanity work area, including the old lavatory, the old wall hanger or vanity, and baseboards.

- Where new electrical or plumbing connections are needed, they have been roughed in at the appropriate locations.

Vanity installation requires the following tools and supplies:

> Magnetic stud finder
> Pencil
> Spirit level
> Power drill and 1/8 inch bit
> Common screwdriver
> Wood screws
> Wood shingles or shims

The above list excludes the vanity and all supplies normally furnished with it.

INSTALLING CABINETS

Vanities

1. Locate and mark two wall studs [1] behind desired vanity location.

2. Remove vanity countertop [4].

3. Move vanity [3] into place against wall.

4. Adjust vanity position until plumb and level, using shims as necessary.

5. Secure vanity to wall with wood screws [2] through frame and into studs.

6. Re-check entire upper surface of vanity frame to assure it is level. Remove high spots and fill in low spots where necessary to provide a good fit with countertop to be installed later.

7. Go to Replacing Lavatories, Page 35.

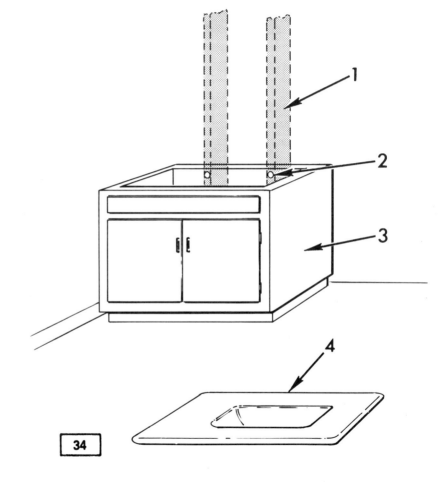

34

REPLACING LAVATORIES

Lavatory replacement is described in terms of six consecutive activities: removing lavatory, removing fittings, installing shut-off valves, installing fittings, installing lavatories, and connecting lavatories.

The procedure covers wall-hung lavatories, lavatories integrated with the vanity counter-top, lavatories mounted from above the counter-top, and lavatories suspended from below the countertop.

Before starting on lavatory replacement, be sure the following things have been done:

- A detailed plan has been prepared specifying lavatory location and height.
- Where the lavatory is to be mounted in a vanity, the vanity base (without the top) has been installed.
- Where the lavatory is to be mounted in a vanity, all required holes have been cut in the countertop.
- All required plumbing connectors have been roughed in at the intended lavatory location.

Also note these important points:

- Where shut-off valves are lacking in the old set-up, plan to install them. Page 38.
- Plan to replace the water supply lines while installing the shut-off valves.

Lavatory replacement requires the following tools and supplies:

>   Magnetic stud finder
>   Pencil
>   Spirit level
>   Pipe wrench
>   Adjustable wrench
>   Common screwdriver
>   Pliers
>   Basin wrench
>   Putty knife
>   Plumbers putty
>   Pipe compound
>   Shut-off valves
>   Flexible connectors. Flexible connectors are corrugated lines which are made so that they can be easily bent. They allow easier hookup between appliances and water supply lines. They are available in different lengths.
>   Wood support. If installing a wall-hung lavatory, a 2 foot length of 1 x 4 board will be required.

The above list excludes tools and supplies required to relocate waste or water source lines. It also excludes the lavatory itself and fittings and components normally obtained with the lavatory.

REPLACING LAVATORIES

Removing Lavatory

For purposes of simplification, the lavatory removal procedure assumes a wall-hung lavatory
without a base cabinet or supporting legs.

1. Turn off water and drain both lines.

2. Remove waste trap [2] from tail pipe [1]
   and empty water from trap into shallow
   pan.

3. Disconnect water supply lines [4] from
   faucet shanks [3] by loosening coupling
   nuts [5] with basin wrench.

CAUTION

Handle tubing carefully to prevent cracking tubes.

4. Lift lavatory away from wall, with fittings
   still attached.

5. If wall hangers will not be needed for new
   lavatory, remove them.

6. Go to Page 37 for instructions for removing
   fittings from lavatory.

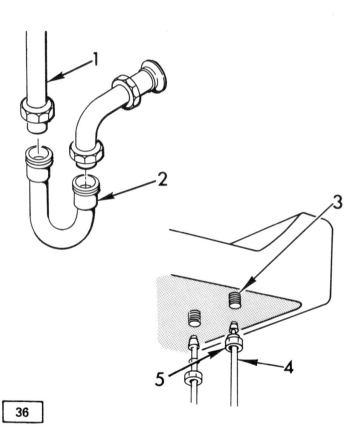

REPLACING LAVATORIES

Removing Fittings

1. Remove locknuts [1] from faucet shanks [2], and lift out faucets.

2. Disconnect lift rod [7] from pop-up assembly [6].

3. Remove pop-up assembly [6] from tail-piece [5].

4. Remove locknut [4] from tailpiece [5] and lift out strainer [3].

5. Remove old putty from all fittings to be re-used.

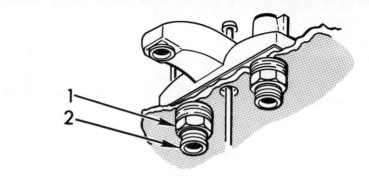

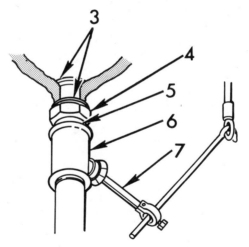

37

REPLACING LAVATORIES

Installing Shut-Off Valves

Each water line requires its own shut-off valve.

1. Disconnect water lines [1] from source pipes [2] in such a way as to leave male threads [3] exposed on source pipes.

2. Attach shut-off valve [4] to each source pipe. Use pipe compound on male threads.

3. Attach flexible connectors [5] to valve outlets.

4. Turn shut-off valves to CLOSED position.

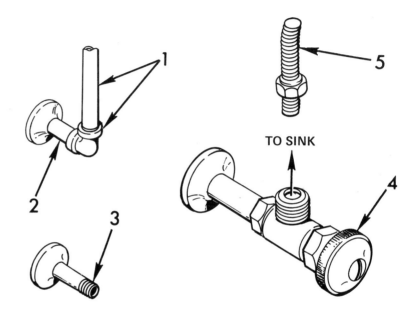

TO SINK

REPLACING LAVATORIES

Installing Fittings

1. Apply plumbers putty around topside of faucet openings [1].

2. Insert faucet shanks [2] through openings.

3. Install metal washer and locknut [3] on each faucet shank.

4. Tighten locknuts [3] and remove excess putty.

5. Apply plumbers putty around topside of drain opening [5].

6. Insert tailpiece [4] through drain opening until flange is flush with lavatory.

7. Install metal washer and locknut [6].

8. Tighten locknut [6] and remove excess putty.

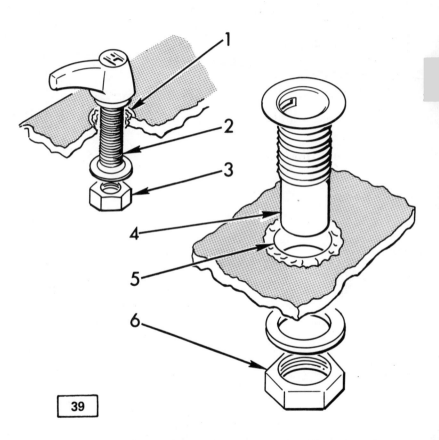

REPLACING LAVATORIES

Installing Fittings

9. Remove stopper [1].

10. Thread pop-up assembly [2] onto tailpiece, using pipe compound to assure watertight fit. When tightening, be sure lift lever [3] points toward rear.

11. Insert stopper [1].

12. Loosely assemble lift lever [3] and pop-up drain rod [4].

13. Set linkage in desired position and tighten setscrew [5].

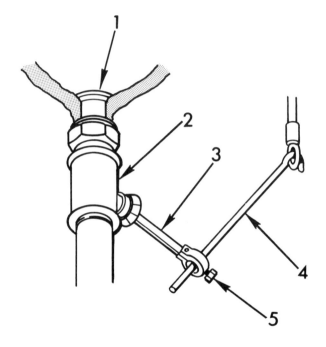

40

REPLACING LAVATORIES

Installing Wall-Hung Lavatory

Where a wall hanger is already installed, go to
Step 8.

1. Locate and mark two wall studs [1] at desired
   sink location.

2. Mark wall between studs to indicate desired
   sink height.

3. Cut into wall and notch studs to accept a
   1 x 4 cross-member [2] flush with stud
   surface.

4. Fasten cross-member to studs with wood
   screws.

5. Bore pilot holes [3] for hanger mounting
   screws.

6. Apply wall finish over cross-member,
   without obscuring hanger screw holes.

7. Mount hanger [4] to cross-member
   with wood screws. Check with level before
   tightening screws.

8. Mount lavatory on hanger.

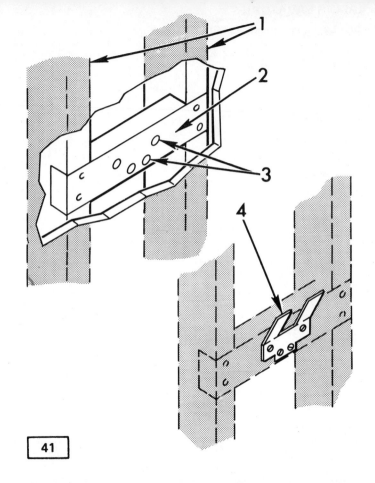

41

REPLACING LAVATORIES

Installing Lavatory Integrated With Countertops

In this arrangement, the countertop and lavatory are built as one continuous unit.

1. Lower lavatory/countertop unit [1] onto vanity cabinet [2].

2. Secure countertop to vanity cabinet with wood screws.

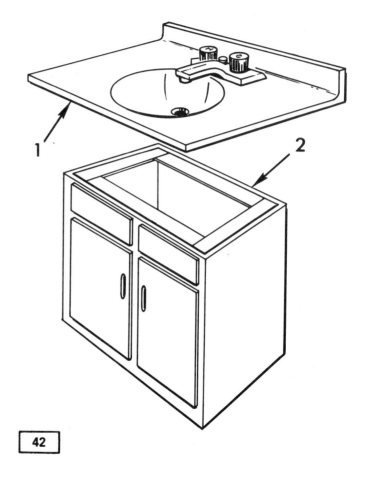

42

REPLACING LAVATORIES

Installing Lavatory From Above Countertop

In this arrangement, the lavatory is mounted in a pre-cut vanity countertop opening by means of a trim ring.

1. Place prefabricated countertop on vanity cabinet.

2. Secure countertop to vanity cabinet with wood screws.

3. Apply plumbers putty to underside of trim ring [6].

4. Place trim ring [1] on lavatory flange [4] and secure by bending tabs [2] inward.

5. Lower lavatory and trim ring into counter-top opening and adjust until even.

6. Insert mounting brackets [5] through slots [3] in trim ring.

7. Secure lavatory to countertop [7] by tight-ening screws on mounting brackets [5].

8. Remove excess putty.

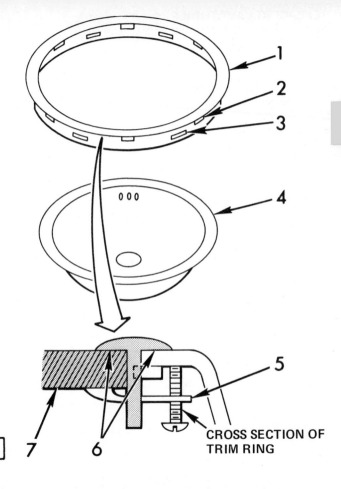

CROSS SECTION OF TRIM RING

43

REPLACING LAVATORIES

Installing Lavatory From Below Countertop

In this arrangement, the lavatory is suspended from a pre-cut vanity countertop opening by means of mounting brackets.

1. Turn countertop upside down and note cabinet mounting holes [1], lavatory cut-out [2], and lavatory mounting holes [3].

2. Place lavatory upside down over lavatory cutout and align by holding lavatory mounting brackets [4] in place temporarily. Trace reference line around lavatory edge.

3. Remove lavatory and apply plumbers putty around edge of lavatory cutout.

4. Place lavatory upside down over lavatory cutout, even with reference line, and press firmly.

5. Install lavatory mounting brackets [4].

6. Remove excess putty inside lavatory.

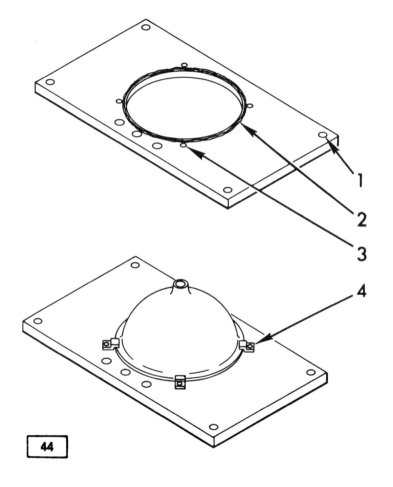

44

REPLACING LAVATORIES

Installing Lavatory From Below Countertop

7. Place countertop [1] on vanity cabinet [3].

8. Secure countertop to vanity cabinet with mounting brackets [2].

9. Install backsplash [5] and endsplash [4] with contact cement.

10. Apply sealant along joints.

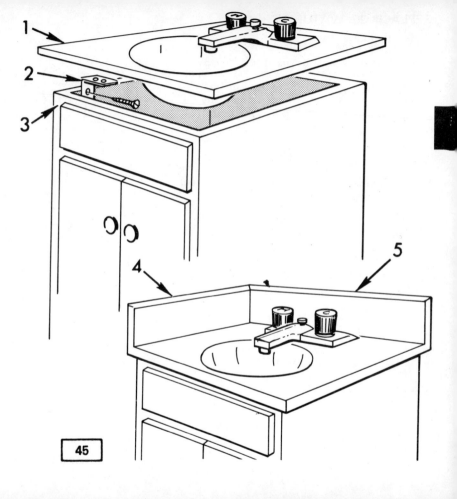

REPLACING LAVATORIES

Connecting Lavatory

Lavatory fittings must be installed. Page 39.

The water supply lines (in the form of flexible connectors) and shut-off valves, are already connected to the source pipes as the result of Installing Shut-off Valves, Page 38.

CAUTION

Handle flexible connectors carefully to prevent cracking them.

1. Gently shape flexible connectors [3] until they align squarely with faucet shanks [1].

2. Attach flexible connectors to faucet shanks. Tighten coupling nuts [2] with basin wrench.

3. Loosely connect trap [5] to waste line and tailpiece. Adjust until properly aligned.

4. Tighten slip joint nuts [4].

5. Turn on water and check for leaks.

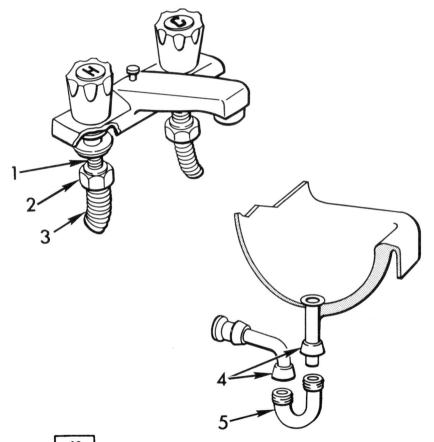

REPLACING TOILETS

Before starting on toilet replacement, be sure the following things have been done:

- A detailed plan has been prepared, specifying toilet location.

- All required plumbing connections have been roughed in at the intended toilet location.

- A closet flange has been installed on the waste pipe to form a solid base of toilet bowl mounting.

Also, note these important points:

- Where a shut-off valve is lacking in the old water supply line, plan to install one. Page 50.

- Plan to replace the water supply line while installing the shut-off valve.

- Plan to replace rubber spud washer in new installation.

Toilet replacement requires the following tools and supplies:

Spirit level
Adjustable wrench
Pipe wrench
Common screwdriver
Pliers
Putty knife
Plumbers putty
Pipe compound
Toilet bowl setting compound
Shut-off valve
Flexible connector
Wax gasket
Rubber spud washer

The above list excludes tools and supplies required to relocate waste or water source lines. It also excludes the toilet itself and fittings and components normally obtained with it.

REPLACING TOILETS

Removing Floor-Mounted Toilet

1. Turn off water, flush toilet, and remove all remaining moisture with sponge or cloth.

2. Remove tank cover and toilet seat.

3. Disconnect water supply line at tank.

4. Remove bolts [1], nuts and washers holding tank to bowl.

5. Lift tank away from bowl and set it aside.

6. Remove spud washer [2] from tank and set it aside.

7. Lift caps [3] and remove nuts and washers from bowl mounting bolts [4].

8. Lift bowl away from bolts and set it aside.

9. Remove old setting compound from closet flange [5] and floor.

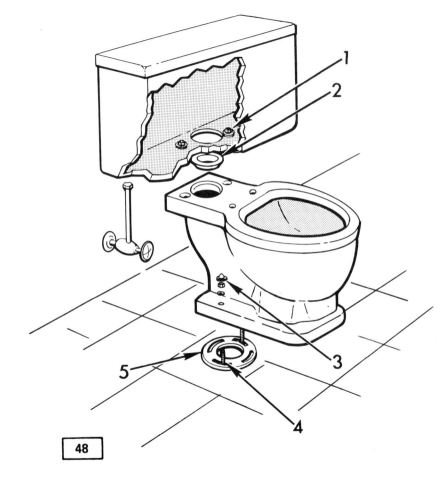

48

REPLACING TOILETS

Removing Wall-Mounted Toilet

1. Turn off water, flush toilet, and remove all remaining moisture with sponge or cloth.

2. Remove tank cover and toilet seat.

3. Disconnect water supply line at tank.

4. Remove bolts [1], nuts and washers holding tank to bowl.

5. Lift tank away from bowl, and set it aside.

6. Remove spud washer [2] from tank.

CAUTION

Have someone else hold bowl during next two steps. Bowl weight may exceed 50 pounds.

7. Remove caps [3], nuts and washers from bowl mounting bolts [4].

8. Lift bowl away from wall, and set it aside.

9. Remove old setting compound from closet flanges [5] and wall.

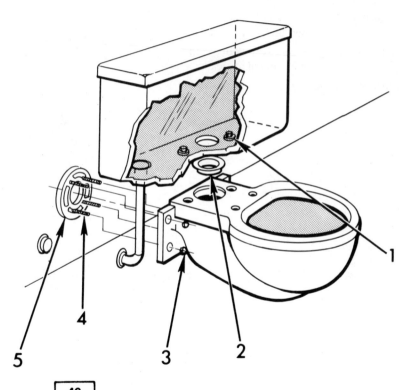

49

REPLACING TOILETS

Installing Shut-Off Valve

1. Disconnect water line [1] from source pipe [2] in such a way as to leave male threads [3] exposed on source pipe.

2. Attach shut-off valve [4] to source pipe. Use pipe compound on male threads.

3. Attach flexible connector [5] to valve outlet.

4. Turn shut-off valve to CLOSED position.

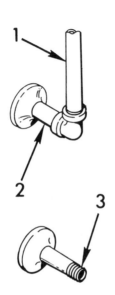

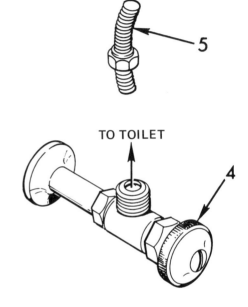

TO TOILET

REPLACING TOILETS

Installing Floor-Mounted Toilet

1. Turn new bowl upside down and press drain gasket [2] around drain opening.

2. Apply 1/8-inch of toilet bowl setting compound around rim [1] of bowl pedestal.

3. Carefully set bowl rightside up on closet flange [3], so that mounting bolts [5] pass through openings in bowl pedestal.

4. Press bowl into place while making it level and properly aligned with walls. Use shims as necessary.

5. Install washers and nuts on mounting bolts [5]. Tighten nuts with fingers.

CAUTION

Tighten nuts carefully. Overtightening can crack bowl.

6. Using wrench, tighten nuts slowly and evenly until bowl feels firm.

7. Remove excess setting compound.

8. Set caps [4] back on mounting bolts with plumbers putty.

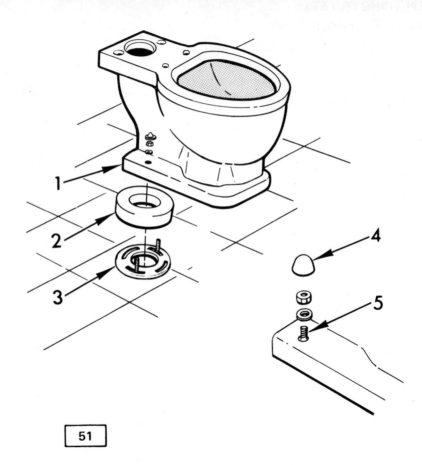

51

REPLACING TOILETS

Installing Floor-Mounted Toilet

9. Install spud washer [3] in tank outlet
    opening [2].

10. Place tank on bowl so that spud washer [3]
    fits evenly into bowl inlet opening [4].

11. Install bolts [1], nuts and washers fastening
    tank to bowl. Rubber washers go inside
    tank. Metal washers go outside tank.
    Tighten nuts with fingers.

<u>CAUTION</u>

**Tighten nuts carefully. Overtightening can
crack bowl or tank.**

12. Using wrench, tighten nuts slowly and evenly
    until assembly feels firm.

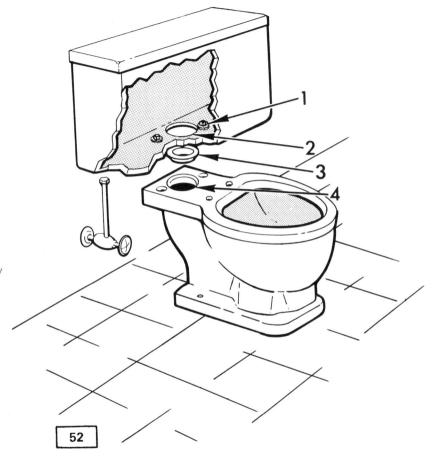

52

REPLACING TOILETS

Installing Wall-Mounted Toilet

1. Press drain gasket [3] around drain opening of bowl.

2. Apply 1/8-inch of toilet bowl setting compound around rim [4] of bowl pedestal.

CAUTION

Have someone help you during next four Steps. Bowl weight may exceed 50 pounds.

3. Carefully set bowl against closet flange [1], so that mounting bolts [2] pass through openings in bowl base.

4. Press bowl into place while making it level.

5. Install washers and nuts on mounting bolts. Tighten nut with fingers.

CAUTION

Tighten nuts carefully. Overtightening can crack bowl.

6. Using wrench, tighten nuts slowly and evenly, until installation feels firm.

7. Remove excess setting compound.

8. Set caps [5] back on mounting bolts with plumbers putty.

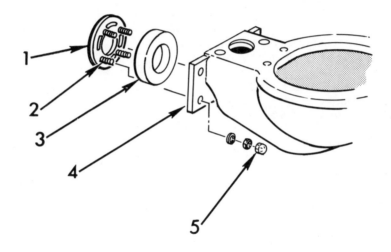

REPLACING TOILETS

Installing Wall-Mounted Toilet

9. Install spud washer [3] in tank outlet opening [1].

10. Place tank on bowl so that spud washer [3] fits evenly into bowl inlet opening [4].

11. Install bolts [2], nuts and washers fastening tank to bowl. Rubber washers go inside tank. Metal washers go outside, underneath bowl ledge. Tighten nuts with fingers.

CAUTION

Tighten nuts carefully. Overtightening can can crack tank or bowl.

12. Using wrench, tighten nuts slowly and evenly until assembly feels firm.

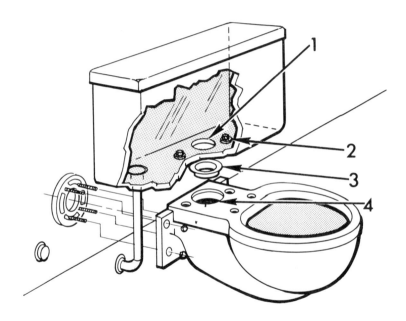

54

REPLACING TOILETS

Connecting Toilet

The water supply line (in the form of a flexible connector) and shut-off valve, are already connected to the source pipe as the result of Installing Shut-off Valve, Page 50.

CAUTION

Handle flexible connector carefully to prevent cracking it.

1. Gently shape flexible connector [3] until it aligns squarely with riser tube shank [1] in tank.

2. Attach flexible connector to riser tube shank. Tighten coupling nuts [2].

3. Turn on water and check for leaks.

4. Install toilet seat and tank cover.

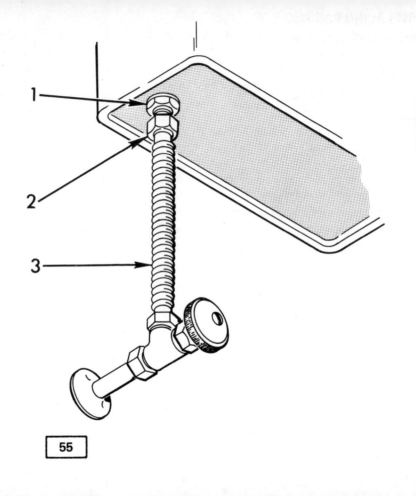

55

REPLACING BATHTUBS

Before starting work on the bathtub, be sure the following things are done:

- A detailed plan has been prepared, specifying tub location and all dimensions relevant to the new arrangement.

- All obstacles have been removed from the tub work area, including the lavatory, the toilet, the vanity, and the wall covering adjacent to the tub.

- Where new plumbing connections are needed, they have been roughed in.

Also, note these important points:

- Bathtub weight may exceed 250 pounds, thus requiring two men to handle it.

- Bathtub length may equal the width of the existing work area. Careful planning will be needed to move the old one out and the new one in without causing damage.

Bathtub replacement requires the following tools and supplies:

Pipe wrench
Adjustable wrench
Socket wrench
Pliers
Claw hammer
Tape measure
Common screwdriver
Putty knife
Power drill and wood bits, 1-1/2 in., 2 in.
Cross cut saw
Pipe compound
Plumbers putty
Wood framing, 2 x 4
Wood supports, 1 x 4
Sealant
Nails

The above list excludes tools and supplies required to relocate the waste or water source lines. It also excludes the bathtub itself and fittings and components normally obtained with it.

REPLACING BATHTUBS

A typical bathtub replacement job has the
following characteristics:

- Old-style tub with faucets/spouts, overflow
  and drain pipes coming through holes in
  tub, and with all pipes exposed.

- Replacement tub with faucets and spout
  passing through holes in wall, and overflow and drain pipes through holes in tub.

- Pipes enclosed in wall, with access opening
  in drain area.

- Wall pipe installation permanent in nature
  including water supply lines [3], faucet
  valve body [2], and plug [1] where
  shower is not to be included.

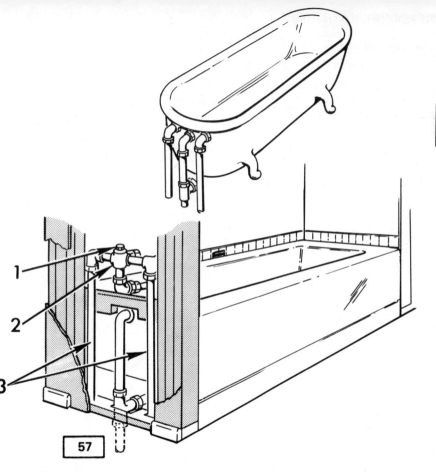

57

REPLACING BATHTUBS

Removing Bathtubs

1. Turn off water and drain both lines.

2. Remove faucets [1] and elbows [3] from water supply lines [5].

3. Disconnect drain tailpiece by loosening slip joint nut [7].

4. Remove overflow pipe [4] by loosening slip joint nuts [2, 6].

The next step requires two men. Bathtub weight may exceed 250 pounds.

5. Lift tub away from wall, leaving only waste pipe connection [9] and water lines [8].

6. Remove old waste pipe connection [9].

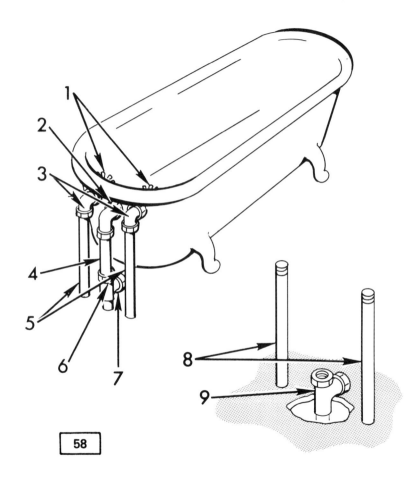

58

REPLACING BATHTUBS

Installing Bathtub

1. Install drain elbow [4] and strainer [3] on tub.

2. Install overflow elbow [11] on tub.

3. Engage stopper mechanism [10] and temporarily install overflow plate [1] on tub.

4. Temporarily connect new waste pipe connection [7] to drain elbow [4] by tightening slip joint nut [5]. Align waste pipe connection with overflow elbow [11].

5. Temporarily connect waste pipe connection [7] with overflow pipe [9], while adjusting length of overflow pipe to fit.

6. Adjust linkage in stopper mechanism [10] to reflect final length of overflow pipe [9]. Lever handle [2] should enable stopper [8] to rise and fall under full control.

7. Disconnect waste pipe connection [7] and install in floor opening [6].

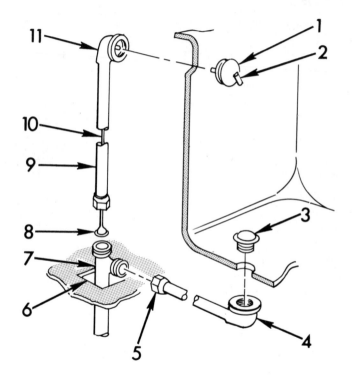

59

REPLACING BATHTUBS

Installing Bathtub

8. Frame in new wall but do not yet install wall covering.

9. Cut notches where necessary for pipes.

10. If building code requires support for your type of tub, nail 1 x 4-inch tub support rails [1] to studs on three walls, at a height just below tub flange.

CAUTION

The next step requires two men. Bathtub weight may exceed 250 pounds.

11. Lower new tub into place.

12. Connect overflow pipe [5] and drain pipe [2] to waste pipe connector [4] by tightening slip joint nuts [3].

13. Extend water supply lines [6] to desired faucet height, leaving ends threaded. Secure pipe to wall structure.

14. Install new faucet body [8] with top plug [9].

15. For tub only, install elbow [7] and nipple [10] leading to spout. (For tub/ shower combinations twin elbow will be used instead. See Installing Tub/ Shower Combinations, Page 65.)

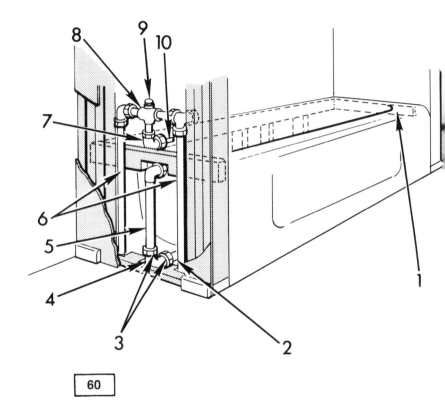

REPLACING BATHTUBS

Installing Bathtubs

16. Temporarily install filter spout and faucets.

17. Turn on water and check for leaks.

18. Remove filler spout and faucets.

19. Finish outside of new wall, leaving access opening [5] for future servicing of waste area. Provide cover [4] for opening.

20. Line inner walls of tub enclosure [1] with waterproof material, leaving 2 inch holes [2] for faucets and a 1-1/2 inch hole [3] for filler spout.

21. Install waterproof sealant along all joints [6] between tub and tub enclosure. Consider using a flexible silicone rubber sealant designed especially for tubs and showers.

22. Install filler spout and faucets.

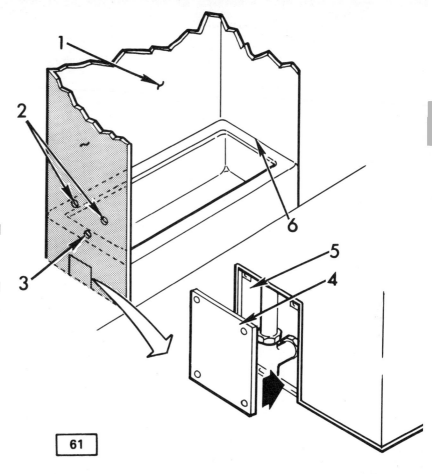

REPLACING BATHTUBS

Replacing Fittings

Bathtub fittings are those parts of the bathtub hardware that are accessible from the tub or tub enclosure inner surface.

Fittings consist of faucets [1], filler spout [2], overflow plate [3], and drain strainer [4].

The filler spout is replaceable without tools.

The overflow plate, drain strainer, and outer parts of the faucet are replaceable with a common screwdriver.

Inner parts of the faucets are replaceable with a socket wrench.

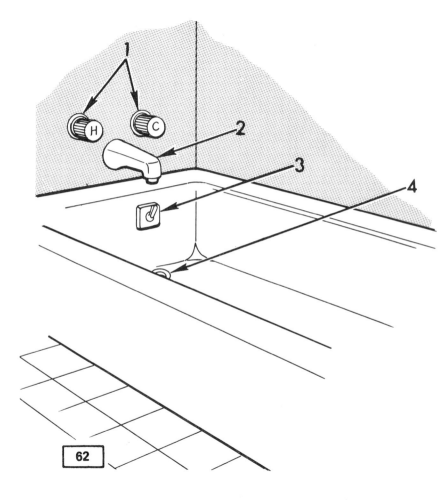

62

REPLACING BATHTUBS

Replacing Filler Spout

1. Unscrew filler spout [2] from spout nipple [1].
2. Screw new filler spout onto spout nipple.

Replacing Drain Strainer

1. Remove drain strainer [4] by removing retainer screw [3].
2. Install new drain strainer and secure with retainer screw.

Replacing Overflow Plate

1. Disconnect overflow plate [7] from tub by removing retainer screws.
2. Withdraw plate [7] about six inches, pulling upper part of stopper mechanism [5] out of opening of tub.
3. Disconnect spring-loaded handle lever [6] from stopper mechanism [5] by removing copper pin [8].
4. Connect new overflow plate [7] to stopper mechanism [5], using cotter pin.
5. Lower stopper mechanism [5] back into place.
6. Secure overflow plate [7] to tub with retainer screws.

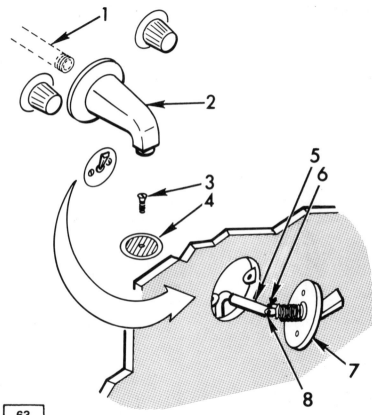

63

REPLACING BATHTUBS

Replacing Faucet

1. Lift faucet plug button [1] and remove mounting screw [2] and handle [3].

2. Unscrew and remove flange [4] and escutcheon nipple [5] to expose valve stem [6] protruding through wall opening.

To reassemble faucet or install a new one, go to Step 5. To replace inner part of faucet, go to Step 3.

3. Using socket wrench, turn nut [8] counterclockwise to remove valve stem/bonnet assembly [7] through wall opening.

4. Using socket wrench on nut [8] install new valve stem/bonnet assembly.

5. Screw on new escutcheon nipple [5] and flange [4].

6. Install handle [3], secure with mounting screw [2] and insert plug button [1].

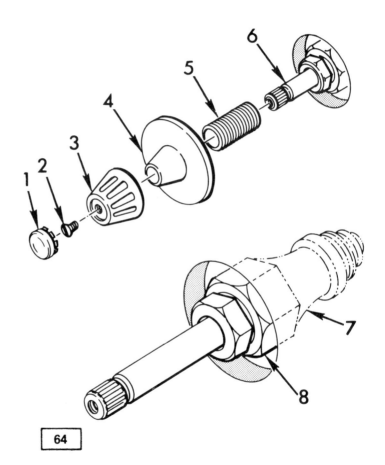

64

INSTALLING TUB/SHOWER COMBINATIONS

Installing a tub/shower combination is similar to installing a bathtub only. The tub/shower combination has four additional major pieces:

Shower head
Diverter spout
Piping to shower head
Shower curtain or sliding glass doors

In order to avoid extensive repetition, the following procedure makes several references to procedures in Replacing Bathtubs, Page 56.

Tub/shower installation requires the following tools and supplies:

Pipe wrench
Adjustable wrench
Socket wrench
Pliers
Claw hammer
Tape measure
Common screwdriver
Putty knife
Power drill and wood bits, 1-1/2 in., 2 in.
Cross-cut saw
Pipe compound
Wood framing, 2 x 4
Wood supports, 1 x 4
Sealant
Nails
Shower head
Diverter spout
Diverter pipe
Shower Curtain

The above list excludes tools and supplies required to relocate the waste or water source lines. It also excludes the tub/shower combination itself and fittings and components normally obtained with it.

INSTALLING TUB/SHOWER COMBINATIONS

1. Remove old bathtub. Page 58.

2. Install new bathtub. Page 59. Perform Steps 1 through 13 only.

3. On pipe [5] install twin ell [3].

4. Install second pipe [2] connecting twin ell [3] to shower elbow [1], six feet six inches above bathroom floor. Anchor shower pipe to wall structure.

5. Temporarily install shower head [6], diverter-type filler spout [4] and faucets.

6. Turn on water and check for leaks.

7. Remove shower head, filler spout and faucets.

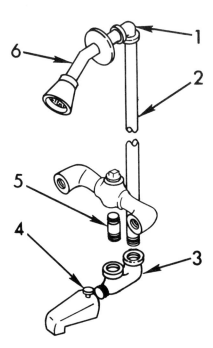

INSTALLING TUB/SHOWER COMBINATIONS

8. Finish outside of new wall, leaving access opening [6] for future servicing of waste area. Provide cover [5] for opening.

9. Line inner walls of tub enclosure [1] with waterproof material, leaving 2 inch holes [3] for faucets, a 1-1/2 inch hole [4] for filler spout, and a 1-1/2 inch hole [2] for shower head.

10. Install waterproof sealant along all joints [7] between tub and tub enclosure. Consider using a flexible silicone rubber sealant designed especially for tubs and showers.

11. Install faucets, filler spout and shower head.

12. Install shower curtain or sliding glass doors.

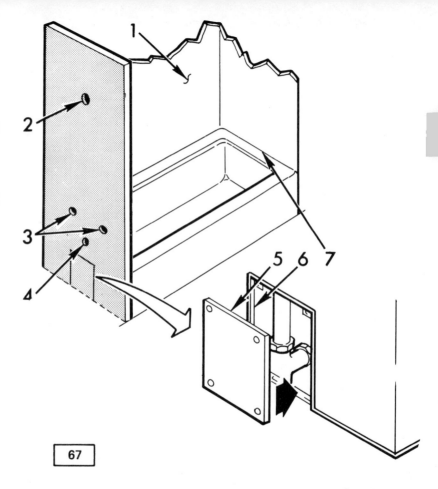

INSTALLING VENTILATORS

Through-the-Wall Ventilators

A typical electrical through-the-wall ventilator consists of an outer sleeve, an inner sleeve, a fan-motor assembly and a shield.

The outer sleeve is inserted into the wall from outside the house; the inner sleeve is forced into the outer sleeve from inside the house. The fan-motor assembly is mounted in the inner sleeve.

A door on the outer sleeve prevents backdraft. The shield covers the inside opening.

Electrical power must be brought to the wall opening through a wall switch.

Through-the-wall ventilator installation requires the following tools and supplies:

>   Magnetic stud finder
>   Tape measure
>   Pencil
>   Spirit level
>   Power drill and bits, 1/8-in., 1/4-in.
>   Keyhole saw
>   Common screwdriver
>   Geometry compass
>   **Masonry shield bits, 1/8-in., 1/4-in.
>   **Hammer
>   **Cold chisel
>   Piece of cardboard larger than interior
>   wall openings
>   *Four expansion anchors or toggle bolts
>   **Four lead anchors

 *For stucco exterior
**For brick exterior

The above list excludes tools and supplies required to install the electrical supply circuit. It also excludes the ventilator itself and components normally furnished with it.

INSTALLING VENTILATORS

Through-the-Wall Ventilators

CAUTION

Be sure to locate studs on each side of opening before cutting into wall. Each edge of opening should be one inch or more away from a stud.

1. Cut opening [1] through inner wall slightly larger than inner sleeve diameter.

2. When outer wall is accessible through finished inner wall opening [1], use cardboard template [3] to locate center [4] on inner surface of outer wall. Mark center point on wall.

3. Bore small hole through outer wall center point [4] from inside. If exterior is stone, brick, or stucco, use masonry drill.

4. Complete cutting of outer wall opening from outside house, using center hole [4] as a guide. Outer opening should be slightly larger than inner opening.

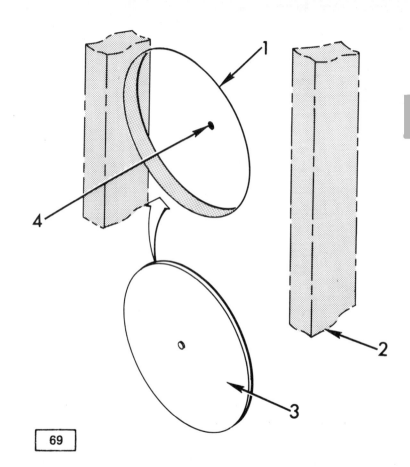

INSTALLING VENTILATORS

Through-the-Wall Ventilators

WARNING

Be sure power is turned off at fuse or circuit breaker box.

5. Have electrical power brought to inner wall opening via conduit [1] through wall switch.

6. Insert inner sleeve [2] into inner wall opening while guiding conduit through hole [3] provided for it. Sleeve flange should be flush with bathroom wall.

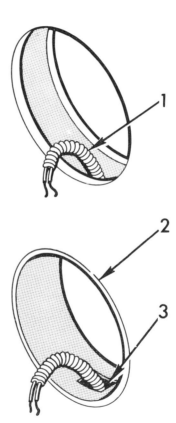

INSTALLING VENTILATORS

Through-the-Wall Ventilators

7. Connect conduit to outlet box supplied with ventilator.

8. Bring house leads into outlet box and connect them to receptacle plug [1].

9. Insert outlet box into hole provided for it and fasten it in place with cover [2].

10. Insert outer sleeve [4] through outer wall opening. Use level to plumb door assembly [5].

11. Mark points [3] where holes will be needed for mounting screws.

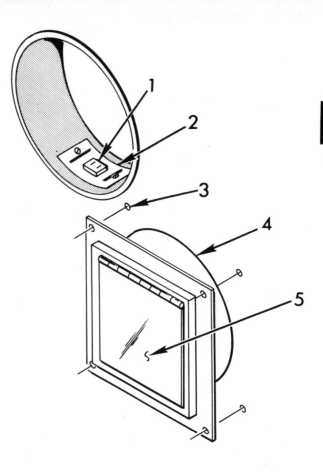

INSTALLING VENTILATORS

Through-the-Wall Ventilators

12. Bore holes for door mounting screws.

   - If exterior is stone, brick or stucco, use masonry drill.

   - If wall is stucco, install toggle bolts [1] or expansion anchors [3] to hold mounting screws. Enlarge holes first.

   - If wall is stone or brick, install lead anchors [2] to hold mounting screws. Enlarge holes first.

13. Fasten outer sleeve door assembly to exterior wall.

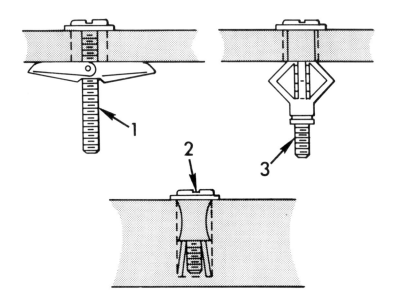

INSTALLING VENTILATORS

Through-the-Wall Ventilators

14. Mount fan-motor assembly [1] on brackets [2] provided in inner sleeve.

15. Install and tighten assembly mounting screws [5].

16. Plug fan-motor power cable [3] into receptacle connector [4].

17. Install shield [6].

18. Turn on power.

19. Use wall switch to verify ventilator operation.

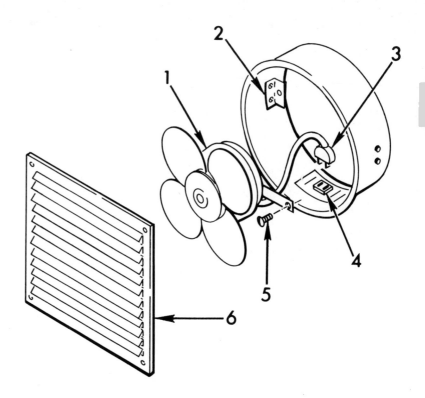

INSTALLING VENTILATORS

Through-the-Ceiling Ventilators

A typical electrical through-the-ceiling ventilator consists of a housing, a fan-motor assembly, and a shield.

The housing is mounted in the ceiling and the fan-motor assembly is mounted in the housing.

The shield covers the ceiling opening when finished.

Electrical power must be brought to the ceiling opening through a wall switch.

Through-the-ceiling ventilator installation requires the following tools and supplies:

Magnetic stud finder
Tape measure
Pencil
Step ladder
Power drill and 1/4-in. bit.
Keyhole saw
Common screwdriver
Extension light

The above list excludes tools and supplies required to install the electrical supply circuit. It also excludes the ventilator itself and components normally furnished with it.

INSTALLING VENTILATORS

Through-the-Ceiling Ventilators

1. Cut opening [2] in ceiling slightly larger than diameter of ventilator housing [5]. Edge of opening should be near enough to joist [1] to allow housing to be fastened to joist for support.

WARNING

Be sure power is turned off at fuse or circuit breaker box.

2. Have electrical power brought to attic side of ceiling opening via conduit [3], through wall switch.

3. Have someone hold housing [5] in opening while you go into attic and fasten housing bracket [4] to joist. Housing flange [6] should be flush with ceiling in bathroom.

Remain in attic for next step, Page 76.

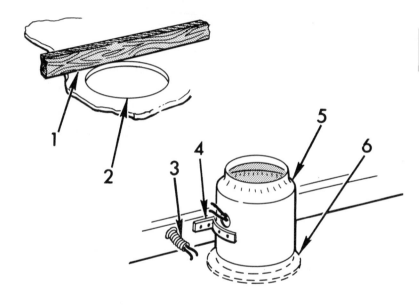

INSTALLING VENTILATORS

Through-the-Ceiling Ventilators

4. Have someone mount fan-motor assembly [2] in housing [1] while you make electrical connection in attic. When connecting house leads [5] to fan-motor leads [4], join white to white and black to black.

This ends attic part of job.

5. Turn on power and use wall switch to verify ventilator operation.

6. Install shield [3] on ceiling opening.

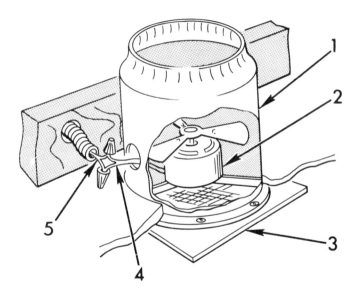

INSTALLING HEATERS

Baseboard Heaters

A typical electrical baseboard heater consists of a heating assembly and a shield.

The heating assembly is surface-mounted at the base of a wall. The shield covers the side of the heater facing the room.

Electrical power must be brought to a point behind the heating assembly through a wall switch.

The heating assembly should be placed high enough above the floor to permit cleaning underneath.

Baseboard heater installation requires the following tools and supplies:

Magnetic stud finder
Pencil
Spirit level
Common screwdriver
Keyhole saw

The above list excludes tools and supplies required to install the electrical supply circuit. It also excludes the heater itself and components normally furnished with it.

INSTALLING HEATERS

Baseboard Heaters

1. Cut opening [1] in wall for junction box [2] to serve heating assembly.

<u>WARNING</u>

Be sure power is turned off at fuse or circuit breaker box.

2. Have independent electrical circuit installed bringing power to wall opening [1] via conduit [3], through wall switch.

3. Terminate conduit in junction box [2] fastened to wall stud.

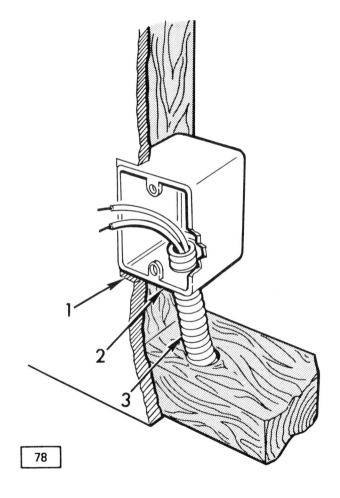

INSTALLING HEATERS

Baseboard Heaters

4. Hold heating element [3] up to wall and pull house leads [2] through hole in heating element.

5. Mount heating element to wall studs [1] in level position.

6. Connect house leads [2] to heating assembly leads [5]. White joins with white. Black joins with black.

7. Install shield [4] with mounting screws [6].

8. Turn on power.

9. Use wall switch to verify heater operation.

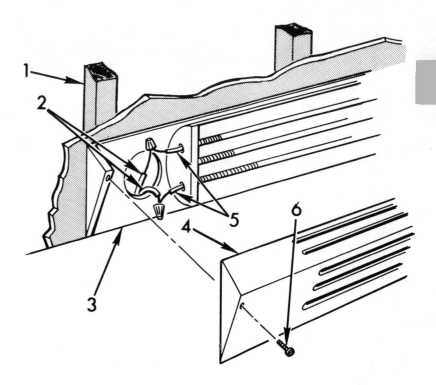

INSTALLING HEATERS

Wall Heaters

A typical electrical wall heater consists of a housing, a heating assembly and a shield.

The housing is mounted in a wall and the heating assembly is mounted in the housing. The shield covers the side of the heater facing the room.

Electrical power must be brought to the wall opening, from which point it is controlled through switches built into the heater.

Wall heater installation requires the following tools and supplies:

Magnetic stud finder
Pencil
Spirit level
Common screwdriver
Keyhole saw

The above list excludes tools and supplies required to install the electrical supply circuit. It also excludes the heater itself and components normally furnished with it.

INSTALLING HEATERS

Wall Heaters

1. Cut opening [2] in wall slightly larger than housing. One edge of opening should be near enough to wall stud [1] to allow housing to be fastened to stud for support.

WARNING

Be sure power is turned off at fuse or circuit breaker box.

2. Have electrical power brought to wall opening via conduit [3] from existing circuit.

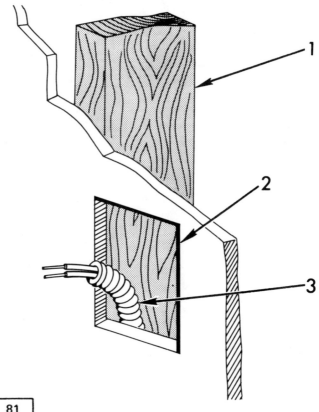

INSTALLING HEATERS

Wall Heaters

3. Pull house leads [1] through hole [3] in housing and secure conduit to housing with locknut [2].

4. Insert housing into wall opening [7] and mount loosely to stud [4]. Housing flanges [6] should be flush with wall.

5. Check with level before tightening mounting screws [5].

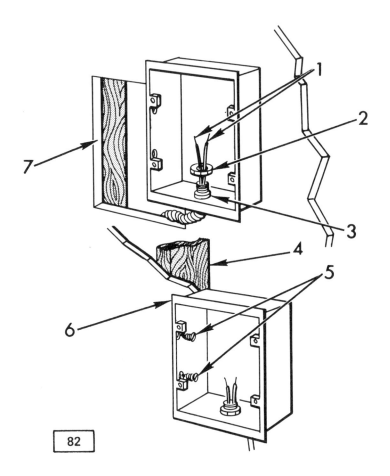

82

INSTALLING HEATERS

Wall Heaters

6. Connect house leads [1] to heating assembly leads [2]. White joins with white. Black joins with black.

INSTALLING HEATERS

Wall Heaters

7. Mount heating assembly [2] in housing with screws [5].

8. Install shield [3] by installing screws [4].

9. Turn on power.

10. Use heater switches [1] to verify heater operation.

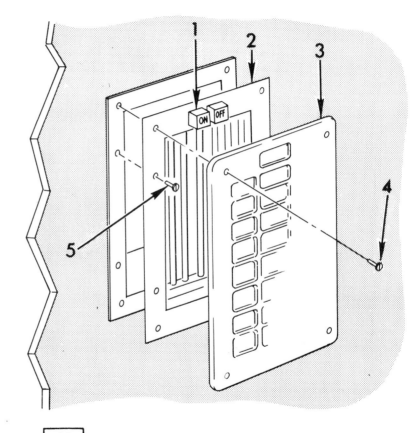

84

INSTALLING HEATERS

Ceiling Heaters

A typical electrical ceiling heater is flush-mounted to a mounting plate, which is secured to a junction box. The junction box is fastened to a ceiling joist.

Electrical power must be brought to the ceiling opening through a wall switch.

Ceiling heater installation requires the following tools and supplies:

Magnetic stud finder
Tape measure
Pencil
Step ladder
Extension light
Common screwdriver

The above list excludes tools and supplies required to install the electrical supply circuit. It also excludes the heater itself and components normally furnished with it.

INSTALLING HEATERS

Ceiling Heaters

1. Cut opening [2] in ceiling slightly larger than junction box [3]. Edge of opening should be near enough to joist [1] to allow junction box to be fastened to joist for support.

WARNING

Be sure power is turned off at fuse or circuit breaker box.

2. Have electrical power brought to attic side of ceiling opening via conduit [4], through wall switch.

3. Terminate conduit in junction box [3] fastened to joist at center of ceiling opening.

This ends attic part of job.

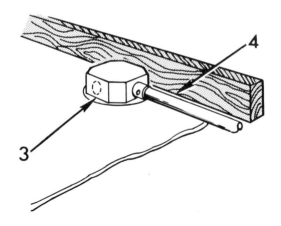

86

INSTALLING HEATERS

Ceiling Heaters

4. Have someone hold heating assembly [5] near opening [1] while you run heating assembly leads [3] through mounting plate [4] and connect them to house leads [2] from junction box. Join white to white and black to black.

5. With someone still holding heating assembly [5], fasten mounting plate [4] to junction box.

6. Fasten heating assembly [5] to mounting plate [4].

7. Turn on power.

8. Use wall switch to verify heater operation.

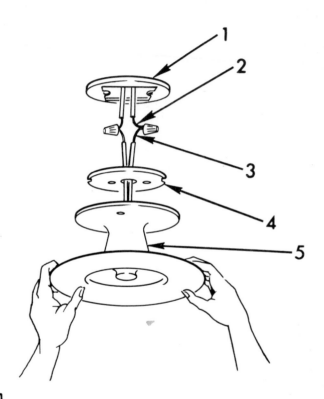

ADJUSTABLE SHELVES

KITCHEN REMODELING

FEATURES OF A GOOD KITCHEN

The kitchen is the center of activity of the home. It is the most-used room in the house, having the most traffic and in many cases serving other purposes than the preparation of meals. Many kitchens are used for family gatherings, washing and ironing, desk work, telephoning, sewing, hobbies, play area, and so on. A dinette or breakfast nook is often included in the kitchen, a useful substitute or addition to the dining room. If so, the kitchen is also a site for meals.

Because of this central position of the kitchen in the family's life and activities, it deserves careful attention to see if it is properly laid out and equipped. Many steps and much reaching and stooping can be eliminated if the kitchen is arranged properly. Moreover, as shown in these "Before" and "After" pictures, the kitchen can be made a very attractive place indeed.

Before you can evaluate *your* kitchen, and determine its good points and bad points, you need to know just what makes a good kitchen. As you discover the specific features that make a good kitchen, you can compare these features against your own kitchen and begin to make plans for modernizing.

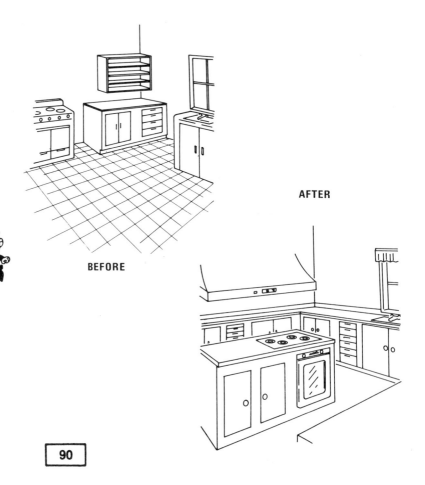

AFTER

BEFORE

90

FEATURES OF A GOOD KITCHEN

General Layout

Even a simple kitchen normally has three separate work areas, or "work centers." There is, first, a work center around the sink, where dishes are washed, vegetables are cleaned, etc. Second, there is a work center around the range, where the cooking takes place. Third, there is a work center around the refrigerator, where items are removed from or placed in cold storage.

A first quick evaluation of a kitchen's layout can be made by connecting these three work centers with lines, as shown in figure A. These lines form what designers and architects refer to as the "work triangle." This is where almost all of the kitchen work occurs. The sides of the triangle, when measured, show how far one must walk between work centers.

Compare the work triangle in figure A with that in figure B. Both kitchens are the same size, but the walking required in kitchen B is much greater than that in kitchen A. Kitchen B has a barrier which must be walked around on every trip from the sink to the range. Yet statistics show that this side of the triangle, from the sink to the range, is the most frequently used path of all. Figure B is an extreme example of poor arrangement, but illustrates a common fault which occurs to lesser degrees in many kitchens.

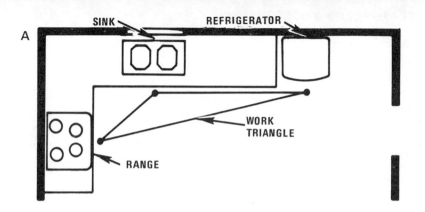

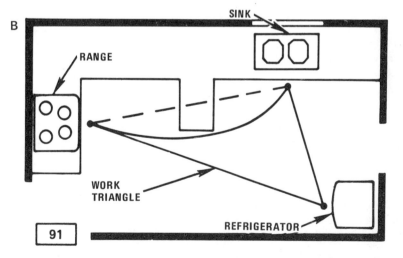

91

FEATURES OF A GOOD KITCHEN

General Layout

The size of the work triangle is thus a good indication of the amount of walking required. The work triangle can also tell us something else. Many kitchens, by virtue of their central location, are subjected to a certain amount of through traffic. The position of the work triangle with respect to this traffic is clearly important. If the traffic passes through the triangle, there will be unnecessary interference and possibly collisions.

Compare the work triangles in figures A and B. While both triangles are compact in size, the traffic in figure B passes right through the work triangle. In figure A, there is no such problem. Traffic can move freely without interfering with kitchen activities.

The position of the doors determine the flow of traffic. If there is interference with the work triangle, either a door may be moved or one or more of the major appliances may be moved. For example, the problem in figure B can be solved in two ways: (1) by moving the door on the right to obtain the arrangement shown in figure A, and (2) by moving the refrigerator to the location marked X in figure B. This is only a simple example to illustrate the important relation between the work triangle and traffic

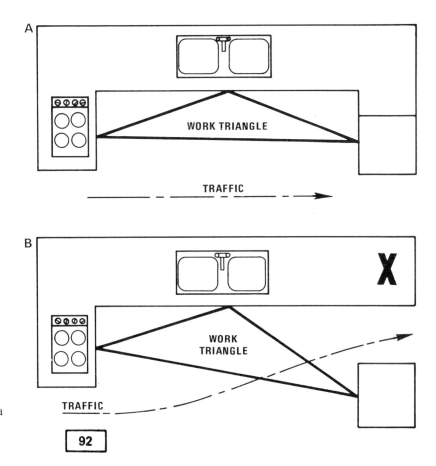

92

FEATURES OF A GOOD KITCHEN

General Layout

flow. The actual solution, of course, will depend also on other factors such as difficulty of moving the door, where the traffic goes to after leaving the kitchen, etc.

Kitchens are usually classified into four basic patterns, as illustrated here. These are U-shaped, L-shaped, single-wall, and corridor (or double wall). None of these patterns is necessarily any better than any other. However, notice that the U-shaped and L-shaped kitchens have work triangles which cannot easily be interfered with by traffic. Both the single-wall and corridor shapes may have an interference problem depending on door location and traffic.

The particular arrangement of sink, range and refrigerator may be different than those shown. These are mainly to illustrate the basic shapes. It is generally desirable that the sink be between the range and the refrigerator, as shown in these examples. The sink area is the food washing and cleanup center, and usually serves also for food mixing and preparation. As the most frequently used work center, it also deserves the central physical location.

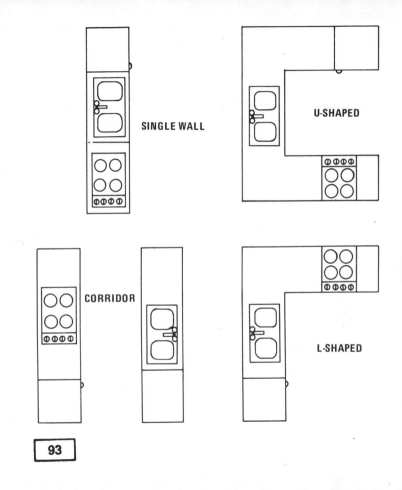

93

FEATURES OF A GOOD KITCHEN

General Layout

These basic diagrams also illustrate another feature of a good kitchen. If there is a window, it usually should be over the sink. A window over the range is not a good idea, as the breeze can blow out the burners of a gas range. Fluttering curtains over the cooking surface of a gas or electrical range can be a safety hazard.

There are many different kinds of kitchen layouts. In particular, there are popular variations on the four basic patterns which have an island or peninsula. An island or peninsula is useful as a room divider, particularly for larger kitchens. It can serve as a work center, snack bar, serving counter, or combination of these.

Here we show a variation of the L-shape, with a corner sink and an island with cooktop and snack bar.

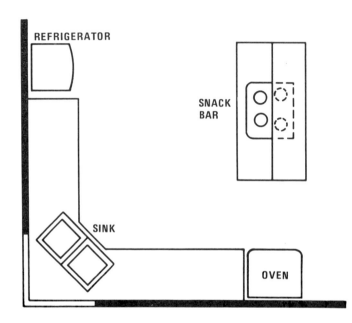

FEATURES OF A GOOD KITCHEN

General Layout

The work centers, as we have seen, should not be too far apart, in order to avoid a lot of walking back and forth. A maximum of about 22 feet is usually prescribed for the total length of the three sides of the work triangle. This is about seven feet between centers, on the average.

It is also important, however, that the work centers not be too confined. As we will see shortly, ample counter and storage space is required around the work centers. This space will not be adequate if the centers are right next to each other. Also, in kitchen arrangements where there are parallel walls, such as the U-shaped or corridor-shaped, there must be adequate distance between the walls. The minimum distance is about four feet. This will allow you to open a drawer or cupboard comfortably without being squeezed against the opposite wall, and will permit another person to pass through if necessary.

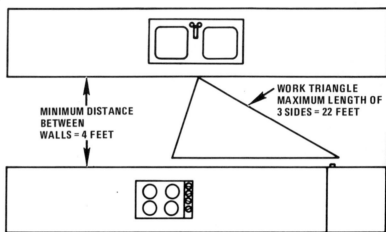

MINIMUM DISTANCE BETWEEN WALLS = 4 FEET

WORK TRIANGLE MAXIMUM LENGTH OF 3 SIDES = 22 FEET

FEATURES OF A GOOD KITCHEN

General Layout

The range should not be installed close against the refrigerator. Not only should there be work space, as mentioned before, but there also needs to be room to avoid heat interference. The range produces heat, and the refrigerator also produces heat, through the rear. The range can interfere with this normal dissipation of heat by the refrigerator, and affect its operation.

For safety reasons, the range should not be placed right next to a doorway, where people could easily brush against it and burn themselves or tip over kettles.

The refrigerator should have the handle on the side next to the work area, as shown in the picture. Then you will not have to walk around the door to get into the refrigerator. Refrigerators are available with the handle on either side. Later, we will discuss in more detail how you should select your refrigerator, range, sink and other appliances.

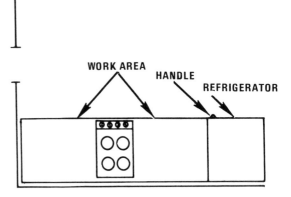

WORK AREA   HANDLE   REFRIGERATOR

FEATURES OF A GOOD KITCHEN

Storage and Work Space

Ample counter space and storage space are essential features of a good kitchen. Moreover, the space must be located where you need it. The following general rules apply:

- There should be counter space on both sides of the sink and on both sides of the range for working areas and for placing or stacking dishes and utensils.

- There should be counter space next to the refrigerator, on the handle side. This is for temporarily placing items while you open or close the refrigerator.

- Storage space for accessories, utensils and small appliances should be provided close to the location where they are used. This means, for example, that storage facilities for pots and pans and other cooking utensils should be within easy reach of the range.

- Cabinets that reach all the way to the ceiling should be avoided unless the space is absolutely necessary. The top shelf will not be used much, and, when it is, you will need a chair or ladder. This could provide a safety hazard.

Later we will consider specific requirements for counter space and storage cabinets in some detail.

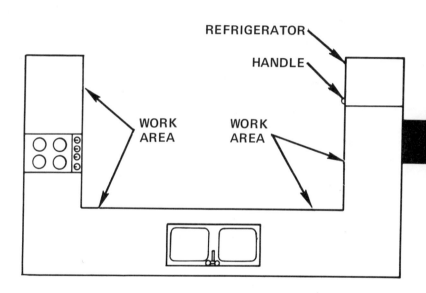

REFRIGERATOR

HANDLE

WORK AREA

WORK AREA

FEATURES OF A GOOD KITCHEN

Lighting and Electrical Outlets

Most kitchens do not have adequate lighting. The work surfaces should not be in shadow. Good lighting is necessary for reading labels and recipes, for adding or measuring ingredients, and for seeing switch positions and temperature and time readings. The choice of lighting can also greatly affect the overall appearance of the kitchen.

Like lighting, electrical wiring and outlets are often inadequate in the kitchen. Nowhere else in the house are there so many appliances, all or most of which may be plugged in at one time. A good margin of capacity is advisable to be able to handle the unusual electrical loads. An electrical range and oven particularly have special electrical requirements.

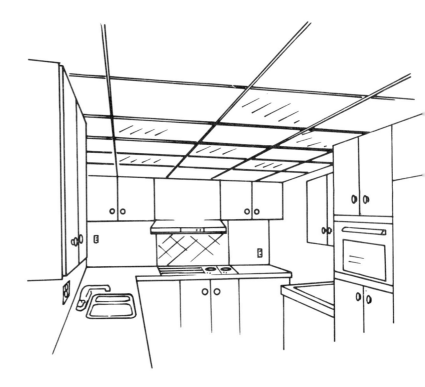

98

FEATURES OF A GOOD KITCHEN

Walls, Floor and Ceiling

Many new and colorful materials have been developed for covering walls, floors and ceilings. For walls, in addition to paint, there are new easy-to-install wallpapers that are moisture and grease resistant. A wide selection of colors and patterns is available.

Tile, fabric and paneling offer other interesting alternatives. For floors, special carpeting is gaining acceptance, and vinyl coverings are now available in cushioned models that are quieter and easier on the feet. Suspended ceilings with recessed lighting afford a welcome change from the older high-ceiling, bleak kitchen. Various kinds of sound-absorbent, easily-installed ceiling tiles are also popular.

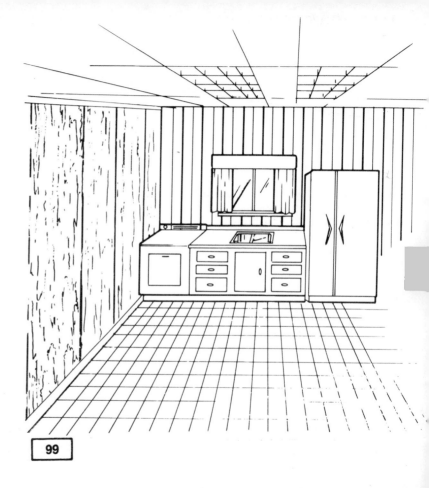

99

SELECTING APPLIANCES

Now that we have had a brief review of the basic features of a good kitchen, we are ready to take a closer look at what kinds of appliances, conveniences, accessories, etc., are available. Since the selection of many of these items will be largely a matter of personal taste, we will emphasize the characteristics to consider in selecting from among the many alternatives.

We will begin with a survey of the major appliances. Corresponding to the three work centers of the work triangle, these include (1) ranges, ovens and cooktops, (2) refrigerator/freezers, and (3) sinks, dishwashers, garbage disposers, and trash compactors. We will consider these in turn.

Ranges, Ovens and Cooktops

There are two fundamental decisions which must be made first in choosing a range. Making these two decisions will narrow the selection to more reasonable proportions. The first decision is whether to have a built-in or free-standing range. The second is whether the range is to be electrical or gas. Often those thinking of remodeling have already made these decisions, but for the benefit of those who haven't the factors in the following pages should be considered.

100

SELECTING APPLIANCES

Ranges, Ovens and Cooktops
Built-Ins Versus Free-Standing

Built-in units give flexibility in placement. The built-in oven can be, and often is, in a separate location from the cooktop surface unit. The oven is used much less than the cooktop, so its proximity to other work centers is less critical. Also, the built-in cooktop often is associated with a pass-through, snack bar, etc. Built-in units can be located at a height to suit you, an important advantage if you are taller or shorter than the average.

Free-standing units are a good choice if you are in a temporary location or if you move often. A compact, free standing unit may also be the best answer to a space problem. These units can stand by themselves or be installed between cabinets. Some examples are shown here. The bilevel type has an oven above the burners and another below. The eyelevel type has the oven above the burners, and the slip-in or drop-in types have the oven below the burners. All of these types are designed to fit closely and integrate well with the surrounding cabinets.

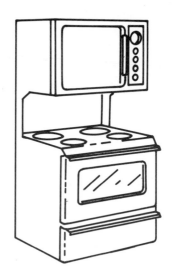

SELECTING APPLIANCES

Ranges, Ovens and Cooktops

Electricity Versus Gas

Many people have a preference for one or the other. Your choice will probably depend on which utility you presently have, as the cost to change can be significant.

Generally speaking, electrical burners take longer to warm up or cool down than gas burners. Contact is more important for electrical burners, so utensils should have flat bottoms. Over a period of time, gas has a tendency to deposit a film on kitchen walls and ceilings. Operating costs for an electrical range are usually somewhat higher than for an equivalent gas range.

From a safety standpoint, you can see a gas flame but the heat of an electrical burner may not be visible. However, almost all electrical ranges now have indicating lights to show which burners are on.

ELECTRICAL

GAS

SELECTING APPLIANCES

Ranges, Ovens and Cooktops

Whether built-in or free standing, and whether gas or electrical, modern ranges incorporate numerous convenience features, both standard and optional. Oven racks are usually adjustable to accommodate different sizes of entrees from a turkey to a pizza. Automatic timers allow you to cook your meal and hold it, a useful feature for those who are frequently away from the house. Many ranges also have an automatically timed electrical outlet for appliances. This can be used for such things as night lights and the morning pot of coffee. Built-in meat thermometers and automatic rotisseries are other commonly available optional.conveniences.

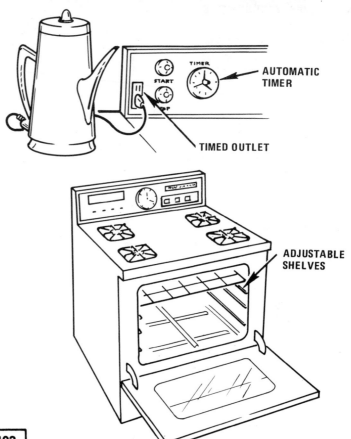

AUTOMATIC TIMER

TIMED OUTLET

ADJUSTABLE SHELVES

103

Ranges, Ovens and Cooktops

Most ovens now come with a self-cleaning feature. There are two types: the self-cleaning (or pyrolitic) oven, and the continuous-cleaning (or catalytic) oven. The self-cleaning oven is cleaned by periodically subjecting it to a high temperature. This changes any food residues to ashes which are easily brushed off. The high temperature is automatically set and timed by a simple knob adjustment.

The continuous-cleaning oven performs a cleaning action continuously while the oven is operating. Chemical action rather than high temperature is the cleaning agent. Chemicals in the oven lining react with food particles, preventing them from sticking and making it easier to wipe the oven clean. Oven doors are usually removable to assist cleaning.

The self-cleaning oven appears to do a generally better job of cleaning than the continuous-cleaning oven. The initial cost of the self-cleaning oven is somewhat higher, but the operating cost is less, because of the better insulation used to cope with the high temperature cycle.

The microwave oven is a new type of oven that can be a useful addition to the modern kitchen. The microwave oven uses electromagnetic waves

to cook food in about one-fourth the time of conventional cooking. Only the food is heated, so the cooking is cooler and cleaner. Metal pots and pans are not used. Cooking is normally done in serving dishes, dinner plates, soup bowls, etc. These normally can be removed without hotpads after cooking.

These units can be plugged into a standard 115 volt outlet, but should have their own circuit. They are normally small portable units, a typical size being 12 inches high by 24 inches wide by 15 inches deep. They can be used as a countertop unit or can be built-in. Some models include built-in kits for this purpose.

Building in presents no fire hazard since the entire unit remains cool, outside and inside.

Those who like their meat brown on the outside should be aware that there are models with special browning elements.

SELECTING APPLIANCES

Ranges, Ovens and Cooktops

In considering different models of ranges or cooktops, look carefully at the location of the controls, from the standpoint of both convenience and safety. Controls at the front can possibly be reached by small children. Controls at the rear, on the backsplash, cannot be reached by children and make for easy cleaning of the cooktop. However, you must reach over hot pans and burners to adjust the controls.

There is usually one burner on the range which has an automatic sensing control. This can be set to cook at a specified temperature. Some ranges have an interchangeable grill, griddle, cutting board or cover for one burner. This may be a large burner for larger cooking vessels. Removable surface units, reflector bowls and trimmings ease the cleaning of cooktops.

An exhaust fan and hood must be installed above the cooktop to remove or filter the hot air. Normally the fan is vented to the outside air but where this is impractical, a non-vented fan with a filter can be used. The bottom edge of the hood should be 24 to 30 inches above the cooktop for maximum effectiveness.

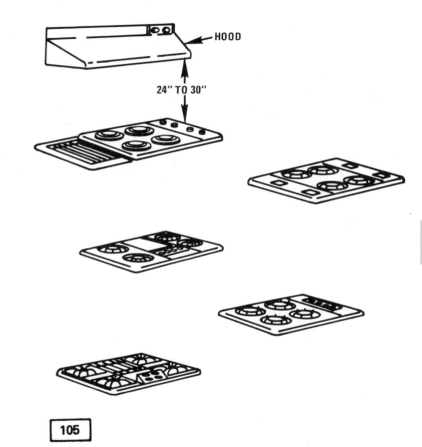

HOOD

24" TO 30"

SELECTING APPLIANCES

Refrigerator/Freezers

In choosing among the different refrigerator/ freezer combinations available, size is the first important consideration. You can make the choice with more confidence if you take note of the following factors affecting size:

- Size of family — a large family requires a large refrigerator. If your family is growing, you may wish to buy a model larger than you presently need, to accommodate future growth.

- Shopping habits — if you shop infrequently, you need more storage space than if you shop daily. If you like to buy vegetables, meat and frozen foods on sale, you should have a large freezer section, or, if you have room, a separate freezer.

Refrigerator/freezers come in single-door and two-door models. The two-door models are the most popular. Some have the freezer on top, some on the bottom, and some have the refrigerator and freezer side-by side. The selection becomes a matter of personal choice. Side-by-side models have somewhat more usable freezer space than the top or bottom models. They also cost more. All are comparable in size for a given capacity.

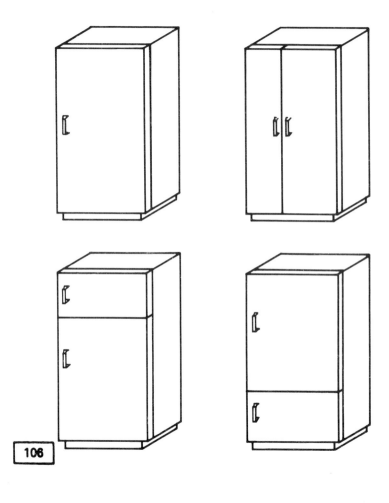

106

SELECTING APPLIANCES

Refrigerator/Freezers

Most important: In whatever model you choose, specify that the door handle be on the side toward the work area. Even in side by side models, remember that you use the refrigerator much more often than the freezer. So specify that the refrigerator handle is toward the work area.

The best temperature to maintain in refrigerator/freezers are 0° in the freezer and 37° in the refrigerator. Some refrigerator/freezers have dual controls, which make it easier to adjust to these optimum temperatures. With a single control, it may be difficult to satisfy both. Most refrigerators have reserve cooling capacity, which becomes important on hot days and as the refrigerator ages.

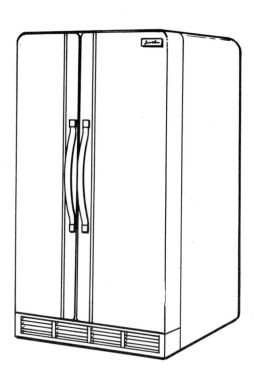

Most refrigerator/freezers are available with a no-frost feature. This is useful in that periodic defrosting becomes unnecessary. The no-frost feature adds to cost, however, both initial cost and operating cost. Also, no-frost models tend to be slightly noisier, and proper packaging is more important to prevent food from drying out.

An automatic ice maker is an optional extra which is convenient if you do much entertaining. It occupies about 1-1/2 cubic feet of freezer

SELECTING APPLIANCES

Refrigerator/Freezers

space, and must be connected to the water supply.

Miscellaneous items to check in selecting your refrigerator/freezer: sliding shelves should have a fence in back to prevent items from falling off. The light bulb should be protected against breakage. Rollers are convenient for moving the refrigerator out for cleaning.

Those who take advantage of meat and grocery sales, or grow their own vegetables, as mentioned before, should consider a large separate freezer.

Freezers come in upright and chest models. The upright model uses less floor space and its contents are more accessible. The chest model holds more food for the same rated capacity, and its temperature is less affected by opening the door.

Temperature has an important influence on the length of time food can be safely frozen. The ideal temperature is 0° throughout the freezer. If the temperature rises to 5° many foods will keep only about one-half as long as they would at 0°.

No-frost models are available as with refrigerator/freezers. Regular models must be defrosted about once or twice a year, depending on the

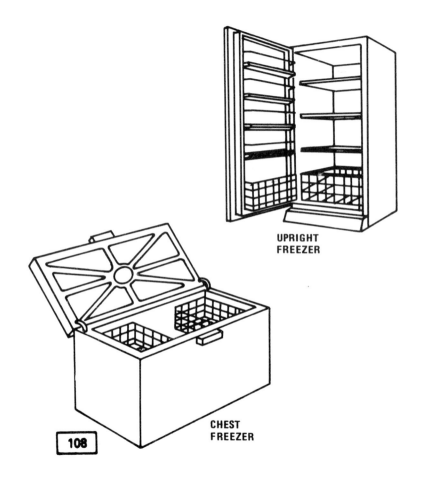

UPRIGHT FREEZER

CHEST FREEZER

108

SELECTING APPLIANCES

Refrigerator/Freezers

humidity and how often the door is opened. Extra care should be taken in wrapping the food for the no-frost model, to prevent food from drying out.

It is a good idea to secure the electrical plug of a freezer with a clamp, to prevent accidental loss of power and a consequent loss of food.

Use a three-wire grounding cord if the freezer is in a sometimes damp area such as garage or basement. If the electrical outlet is controlled by a switch, the switch should be removed or taped closed.

For proper operation, your freezer or refrigerator/freezer should be level. Also, check that there is room for air circulation around the unit. An added precaution: if there is a possibility of children getting into your freezer, use a lock.

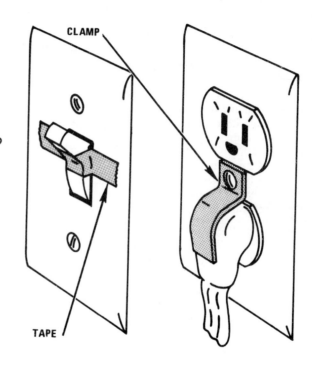

SELECTING APPLIANCES

Sinks and Related Items

The area around the sink is the cleanup center and is the logical location for some of the newer appliances such as dishwasher, garbage disposer and trash compactor.

Sink: The sink itself is available in a variety of color-coordinated enamel finishes, or in stainless steel. The standard sink has a single compartment, but increasingly in demand are sinks with double and even triple compartments. Often one of the compartments is small and is meant for the garbage disposer. For example, a double sink may have a smaller, shallower central disposer compartment.

A wide range of attachments adds to the convenience of the modern sink: cutting board tops, spray attachments, liquid detergent dispensers, hose and brush attachments, hand lotion, etc.

Fixtures are available with single lever arms for mixing hot and cold water, and swivel spouts for reaching each compartment.

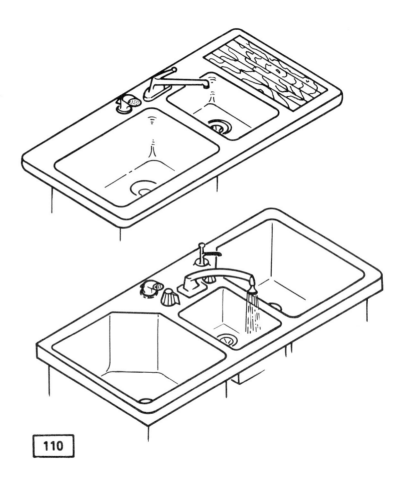

SELECTING APPLIANCES

Sinks and Related Items

Dishwasher: The automatic dishwasher makes the cleaning of dishes much easier than it used to be. The diswasher can handle large loads if necessary — as many as 13 place settings in some models. Or, if the family is small, the dishes can be stored out of sight in the dishwasher and put through a short rinse cycle. The full cycle can then be used when the load warrants.

Depending on your needs, you can select from four models:

- Built-in — installed under the counter, and opens from the front
- Free-standing — front or top loading. The top serves as a work surface
- Portable — front or top loading. Can be moved out of the way after cleaning dishes
- Portable/convertible — front loading only. Can be used as portable, and later built-in.

All models are 24 inches wide. The built-in is 34-1/2 inches high, to allow it to fit under a 36 inch counter. The other three models are 36 inches high. When the portable/convertible is installed, the top is removed so that it fits under the counter.

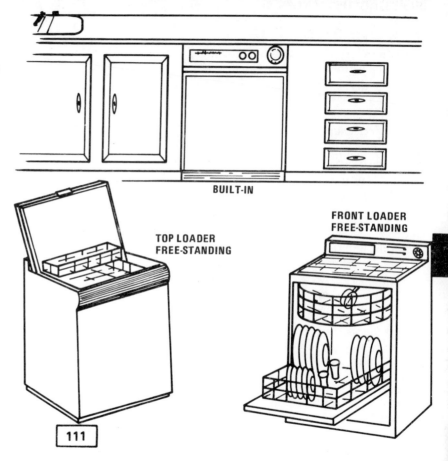

BUILT-IN

TOP LOADER FREE-STANDING

FRONT LOADER FREE-STANDING

111

SELECTING APPLIANCES

Sinks and Related Items

Dishwashers vary in the kinds of automatic cycles they perform. In selecting a dishwasher, you should choose the cycles which you will use.

Heat and strong detergent are capable of damaging certain plastic items, fragile crystal, etc. Examples of the cycles available are:

- Regular or Short Cycle — for normal loads
- Super Wash — for hard-to-clean items such as pots and pans
- China Crystal — for delicate or valuable items
- Rinse and Hold — for storing dishes for future washing
- Rinse Dry — for dusty dishes, drinking glasses, etc.

Most machines have a rinse conditioner, which reduces the spotting caused by hard water. The amount of water used in a normal cycle is 12-16 gallons. In an area where water is in short supply, or where there is a sewage or drainage problem, this should be taken into account. Also, since dishwashers have a timed fill, a low water pressure can cause problems.

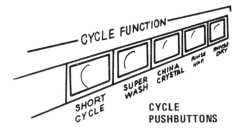

CYCLE
PUSHBUTTONS

RINSE
CONDITIONER
DISPENSER

Sinks and Related Items

Some machines have a blower for drying and some do not. Drying is usually more efficient for machines with blowers.

Garbage Disposer: Most food except for large bones can be conveniently flushed down the garbage disposer. Some models grind everything easily, whereas others may require special handling — slow feeding, much water, and mixing with other garbage — for such tough items as corn husks. All disposers have provision for connection to the dishwasher drain, so that remnants from dishwashing will pass through the disposer.

There are two types of garbage disposer, the batch-feed and the continuous-feed. The batch-feed is run only after it is filled and the stopper is locked in the drain position. The continuous-feed is operated continuously while garbage is being flushed into it, and is turned on and off with a switch. The batch-feed is designed for safety, but may be a nuisance in disposing of large quantities of food.

Some models are noisier than others, which is not necessarily a disadvantage. In fact, some are so quiet that it is advisable to have a signal light to remind you they are on.

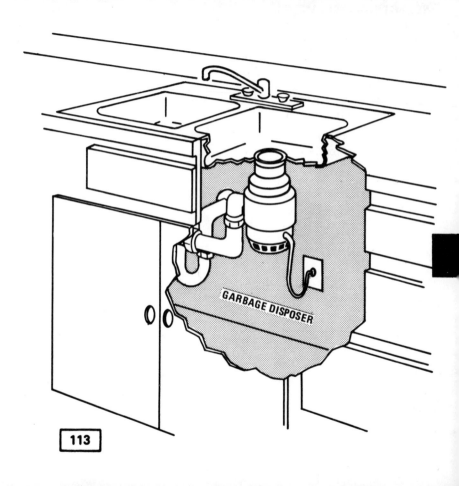

GARBAGE DISPOSER

113

Sinks and Related Items

Garbage disposers use a lot of water, which is a factor in arid areas. Your local ordinances should be checked to make sure disposers are permitted. If you have a septic tank or cesspool, they may not be allowed.

For safety, the on-off switch for continuous-feed garbage disposers should be located at a distance from the disposer. The minimum distance should be about six feet, to prevent a person from reaching the switch while feeding the disposer.

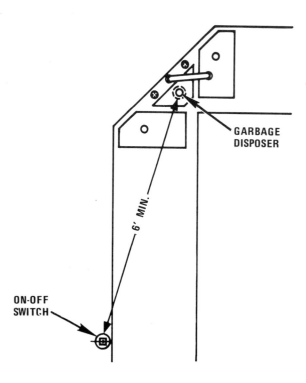

GARBAGE DISPOSER

6' MIN.

ON-OFF SWITCH

SELECTING APPLIANCES

Sinks and Related Items

Trash Compactor: The most recent addition to the appliance line is the trash compactor. This device will compress and store a week's trash for a family of four. It is loaded non-selectively with cans, bottles, paper, etc., which it then crushes and deodorizes. At the end of the week, a neat package is ready for pick-up.

The trash compactor is available in both built-in and free-standing models. Little space is required, as the unit is only 15 inches wide. Like a dishwasher, the built-in model will fit neatly under the countertop, usually in the sink area.

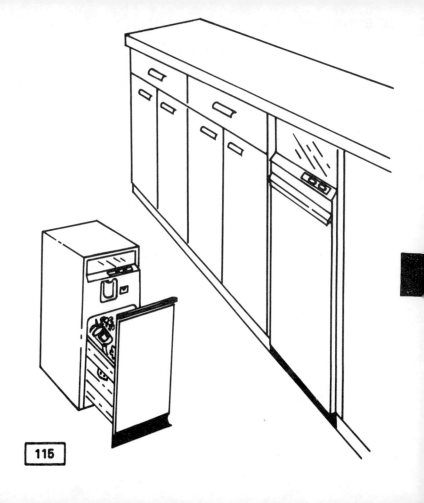

115

SELECTING APPLIANCES

We have seen what is available in the way of new appliances and some of the good and bad characteristics to look for. Before buying, however, you should try to see some of the actual appliances. To do this you can tour manufacturers' showrooms, or visit large department stores or appliance dealers.

As you shop, make a list showing manufacturer's name and model number, price, delivery cost, and installation cost. Check guarantees and warranties, to find out what it will cost if something goes wrong. Many freezer manufacturers, for example, will give you free insurance covering the food in your freezer, in case of a freezer failure.

A good source of information is friends who have appliances with features similar to those you are considering. Find out if they are satisfied and if they believe the special features or conveniences were worth the extra cost.

MFG	MODEL	PRICE	DEL. COST	INST. COST

STORAGE AND WORK SPACE

A well-designed kitchen has ample storage space which is both easily accessible and balanced as to type of storage. Many cupboards and few drawers, or vice versa, will prove unsatisfactory for most kitchens. Deep corner cabinets or shelves near the ceiling are also undesirable. Accessibility is also the key in planning counter space. Long stretches of countertop away from the work centers will be of less use than more modest work space near the sink, refrigerator and range.

In addition to being functional, cabinets and countertops, when properly selected and integrated with modern appliances, make for a truly attractive kitchen. Later we will see how wall, ceiling and floor coverings also contribute to the overall effect.

Let us now look at some of the specifics you'll need to consider in selecting and locating cabinets and counterspace in your kitchen.

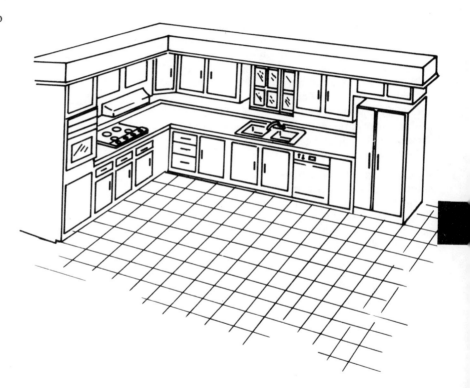

STORAGE AND WORK SPACE

Cabinets

Kitchen cabinets can be bought ready-made, finished or unfinished, or, if you wish, you may have custom cabinets built to order. Ready-made cabinets are available in a range of sizes, sufficient to satisfy normal requirements. Both natural wood and steel cabinets are on the market. Only if you have some unusual space problem, or want some particular, unique finish, should you consider custom cabinets. The difference in cost is large.

In discussing cabinet dimensions and other characteristics we must, of course, first distinguish between wall and base cabinets. Standard wall cabinets, as shown here in profile view, are only half as deep as base cabinets. Wall cabinets are usually 12 inches deep, and base cabinets, 24 inches deep. Base cabinets of greater depth would make it more difficult to reach items stored in back, and would also interfere with reaching wall cabinet shelves.

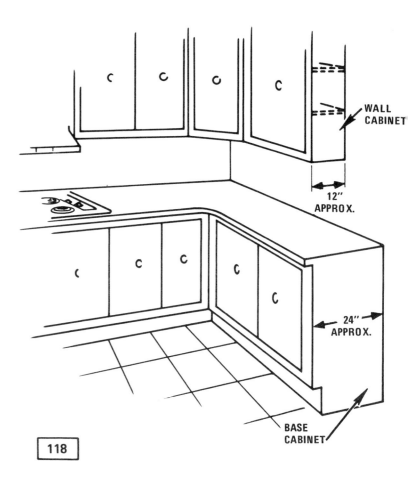

WALL CABINET

12"
APPROX.

24"
APPROX.

BASE CABINET

118

STORAGE AND WORK SPACE

Cabinets

Shown here are other typical dimensions of ready-made wall and base cabinets. When the base cabinet is under open counter space, as shown here, there are normally 15-to-18 inches between the counter and the bottom of the wall cabinet to allow working room. The height of the wall cabinet is 30 inches here, but will differ for cabinets over the sink, range, or refrigerator, as we will see.

The wall cabinet usually does not reach to the ceiling, as the top shelf would then be inaccessible without a ladder. Instead, a soffit is commonly used to fill space above the cabinet. The soffit can be decorative and is useful for indirect lighting or to hide ducting.

Ready-made cabinets are available in widths from 12 inches to 60 inches. A width of 30 to 36 inches is most popular. Those 21 inches wide or less usually have only one door, so you will want to specify a left-or right-hand door, as with the refrigerator.

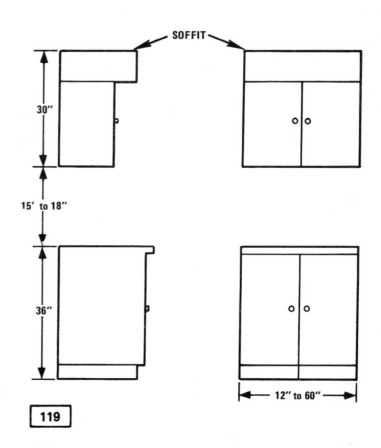

119

STORAGE AND WORK SPACE

Cabinets

Over a range, the bottom of the wall cabinet should be about 30 inches above the burners. Normally, a range hood will be installed on the cabinet, as shown. Typically, the distance between hood and range top will be about 24 inches to allow room for maneuvering. A popular height for cabinets over ranges is 18 inches. A 15-inch height is normally used over the refrigerator. The size of cabinet, if any, over the sink may depend on the presence of windows, but the 15 and 18 inch heights are often used here too.

Standard base cabinets are available for installing sinks or cooktops. These have a floor and sides and, sometimes, a back. Widths of 24 inches to 42 inches are the most popular. There are also wall cabinets for standard ovens or double ovens. Most common are 24-to-30 inch widths.

The kitchen, overall, should have a total frontage of at least ten feet of wall cabinets, and about the same amount of base cabinets, for adequate storage. In planning your cabinet locations, do not feel it is necessary to place cabinets of equal width on each side of the sink or the range. It seldom works out that way.

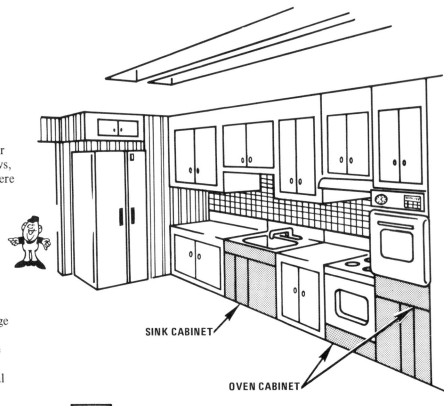

SINK CABINET

OVEN CABINET

STORAGE AND WORK SPACE

Cabinets

Wall cabinets are usually cupboard type, some with adjustable shelves. Base cabinets may be of either the cupboard or drawer type, or a combination of both. In planning your kitchen, keep in mind that nine drawers are considered about right for most kitchens.

In the area near the sink, it is common to place base cabinets with one or two drawers above and a cupboard below. The drawers are a handy repository for silverware and other small utensils.

A very popular feature in base cabinets is slide-out shelves. These eliminate much of the stooping and groping for items in the rear. For corners, a base cabinet or wall cabinet with a built-in lazy susan or swing-out shelves makes the entire corner useful and easily accessible.

If cabinets in the standard sizes do not exactly fit the space available, you can buy matching filler strips up to three inches in width to make a snug fit. End cabinets which will not be against a wall should be ordered with a finished side on the exposed end.

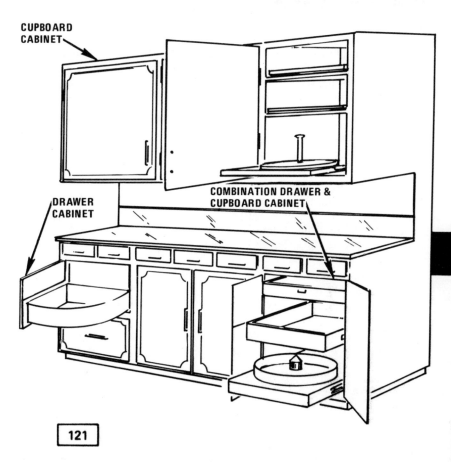

CUPBOARD CABINET

DRAWER CABINET

COMBINATION DRAWER & CUPBOARD CABINET

121

STORAGE AND WORK SPACE

Cabinets

Other special cabinets that you should be aware of in your planning are cabinets with swing-out doors for spices and other small jars, cabinets with vertical tray storage for cookie sheets, trays and platters, and cabinets with built-in mixer units, built-in chopping block tops or heat-resistant tops. For islands or peninsulas, both base and wall cabinets are available with doors on both sides. The wall cabinets must be suspended from the ceiling.

For kitchens without a separate pantry, tall pantry cabinets are available that are three feet wide and two feet deep. Complete with shelves and pivoting racks, these have a large capacity all of which is easily accessible.

If you need to increase the storage capacity of your cabinets without increasing their size, consider using small auxiliary shelves above and behind existing shelves, for small items. Also, peg-board or hooks on the inside of cabinet doors can be useful for utensils, knives, spatulas, etc.

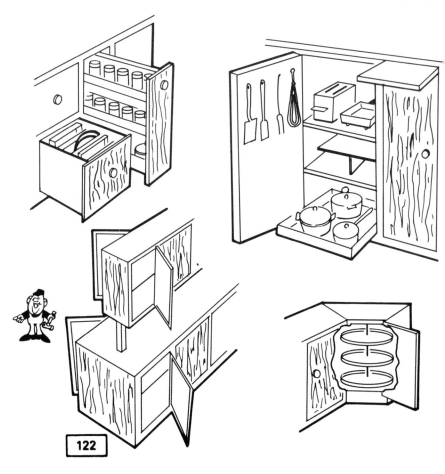

122

STORAGE AND WORK SPACE

Countertops

As with cabinets, countertops are available in ready-made form or can be custom-ordered. Tile countertops, of course, must be built in place. Tile and plastic laminates are the most common counter surfaces. Readymade countertops normally include the backsplash, on the wall between counter and wall cabinets. They also come with the sink or cooktop cutout already made.

It is important to first recognize commonly accepted minimum work or "set down" space at the work counters. These are:

- Range — provide at least 15 inches on each side of the cooktop, and 24 inches on one side of a wall-mounted oven. These need not all be separate; that is, if the 24 inches of "set-down" space for the oven also happens to be one side of the cooktop, there need not be an additional 15 inches for the cooktop on that side.

- Refrigerator — provide at least 18 inches next to the handle side of the refrigerator

- Sink — provide at least 18 inches on each side of the sink. There should be at least 36 inches of uninterrupted surface for the mixing center. If this is on one side of the sink, there need not be an additional 18 inches on this side for the sink.

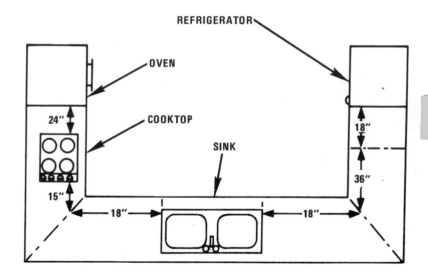

STORAGE AND WORK SPACE

Countertops

If you find you need counter space, consider installing an island or peninsula. These also serve as room dividers, while maintaining an opening for communication between the rooms. The opening over a cooktop, for example, furnishes a handy pass-through to the dining area or adjoining snack bar.

Another possibility to increase counter space is to use a triangular or curved form instead of strictly rectangular. This would, however, require a custom design.

Standard height of the counter is 36 inches. Depending on what is comfortable for you, this height can be increased or decreased an inch or two by raising or lowering the base cabinets. Lowering is accomplished by reducing the toe space below the cabinets.

Work surfaces have been found to be most comfortable when they are two-to-six inches below the elbow. For most people, a 36-inch height is satisfactory. However, for such tasks as chopping, or kneading and rolling dough, 32 inches is a more comfortable height for most people. For this reason, you may want a separate table or pull-out if you do these things frequently.

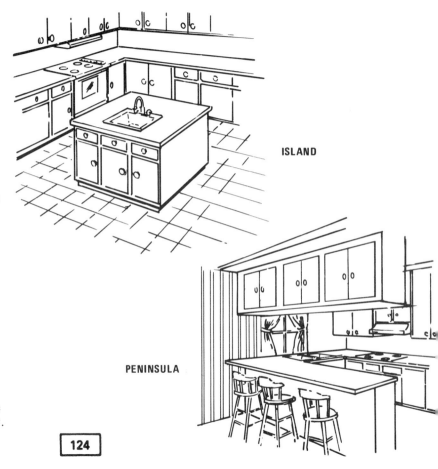

ISLAND

PENINSULA

124

LIGHTING AND ELECTRICAL OUTLETS

These are two areas where many kitchens are deficient. While you are remodeling is a good time to look at your kitchen critically from the standpoint of quantity and quality of lighting and adequacy of electrical wiring.

Kitchen lighting should be considered in two parts, overall area lighting and work center or task lighting. The area lighting consists of ceiling and/or wall fixtures which light the whole room and contribute to its general appearance and attractiveness. In addition, you need good lighting at each work center so that you are not working in a shadow. Under-cabinet lighting is often convenient for this purpose.

Depending on personal preference, incandescent or fluorescent bulbs may be used. Fluorescents consume somewhat less electricity. Fluorescents come in "warm" or "cool" types. The Warm White Deluxe (WWX) fluorescents enhance the appearance of many foods, as well as warm fabrics and paints, and complexions. If you intend to combine incandescents and fluorescents, WWX is recommended. Cool White Deluxe (CWX) fluorescents simulate natural daylight, and work well with cool colors.

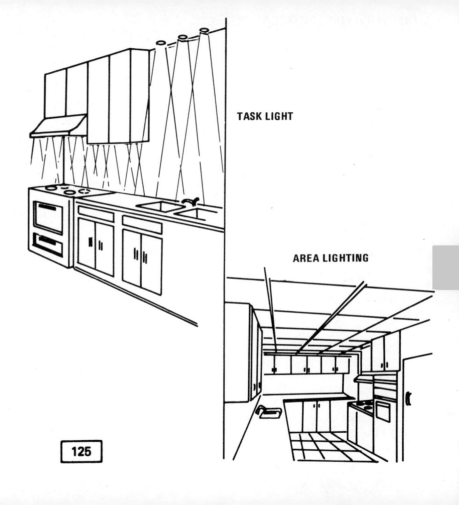

TASK LIGHT

AREA LIGHTING

125

LIGHTING AND ELECTRICAL OUTLETS

Lighting requirements depend on the individual kitchen. A kitchen with a white ceiling, for example, requires less light than one with a dark ceiling. An average kitchen might require about 200 watts of incandescent bulbs or four 40-watt fluorescent tubes for general lighting, plus lighting at the work centers. For example, you might have two 30-watt fluorscent tubes over the sink and one 30-watt tube over the range.

There should be a light switch for the general lighting at each entrance to your kitchen, if there is more than one entrance.

To accommodate the many portable appliances now used in the kitchen, you'll need a sufficient number of receptacles with sufficient power-handling capacity. You may be purchasing new small appliances in the future, so it is well to have some reserve capacity. Even the new microwave ovens, for example, are plug-in, countertop units (although they may also be built-in).

As a general rule, provide one duplex receptacle for each four feet of counter frontage. This means that you will have at least two, and perhaps three, such receptacles. At least two separate 15-20 amp circuits should be provided

for these outlets. Your electrical contractor will help you in determining these requirements.

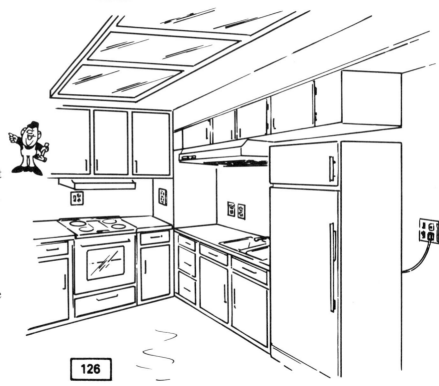

126

WALLS, FLOOR AND CEILING

Often the most remarkable changes in the over-all appearance of the kitchen are achieved through new treatments or coverings on the walls, floor and/or ceiling. Because the homeowner can usually do much of the work himself, there is extra satisfaction in the results, and they are realized at less expense than many of the other remodeling tasks.

Wall Coverings

The most common wall treatment by far is, of course, paint, but the many new materials avail-able in wallpaper, tile and paneling should also be given some consideration before deciding. On certain areas even pegboard, or brick or stone, may be the finish your kitchen needs.

If you plan to paint, enamel is best for the kitchen because it is durable and easily wiped clean. Either an oil-based or water-based enamel will do. A good oil-based enamel will generally last longer but a water-based paint is easier to work with.

Moisture-proof wallpapers with bold patterns and striking colors are now on the market. These are easily washable and entirely suit-able for the kitchen. The new pre-pasted wall-papers are easy to apply.

127

WALLS, FLOOR AND CEILING

Wall Coverings

Paneling is becoming more popular in the kitchen. It is often used in combination with paint or wallpaper. There is an extraordinary variety of materials and finishes to choose from. Wood veneers and solid wood are widely used. Even more suitable for the kitchen are the plastic laminates, similar to that used for counter tops. These are easy to install, are very durable and can be wiped clean easily.

Wall tiles of plastic and metal are another available option. Cracks between the tiles are sometimes difficult to avoid, however, and these can lead to deterioration when exposed to kitchen moisture and grease.

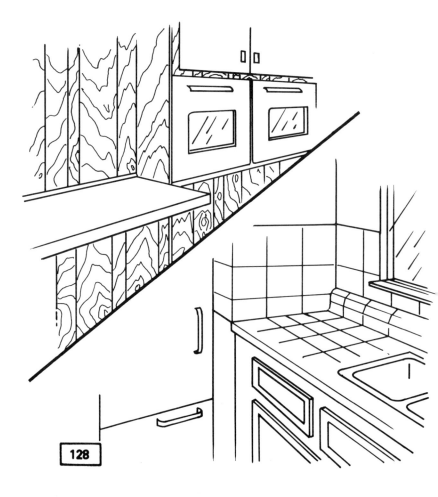

128

WALLS, FLOOR AND CEILING

Floor Coverings

It is easy to install floor coverings with many of the new materials available provided the original floor is reasonably smooth and solid. Bumps and depressions will tend to show through a new floor covering in time, however, so if there are irregularities, patch them or plan on laying a foundation surface of plywood or hardboard.

The most popular kitchen floor covering is undoubtedly vinyl, in sheet or tile form. With sheet vinyl, there are no cracks between tiles to worry about. However, it is more expensive than tiles, and more difficult to install for the inexperienced. Sheet vinyl is now available in a cushioned form, which has a resilient layer sandwiched between the wear surface and backing. Cushioned sheet vinyl, while more expensive, is easy on the feet, has excellent durability to withstand the heavy kitchen traffic, and is less likely to break dropped items.

There is a wide variety of colors and designs available in sheet vinyl. Cost will vary to some extent depending on popularity of the model and intricacy of the design. Most come in six-foot wide rolls which must be cut to size by the dealer.

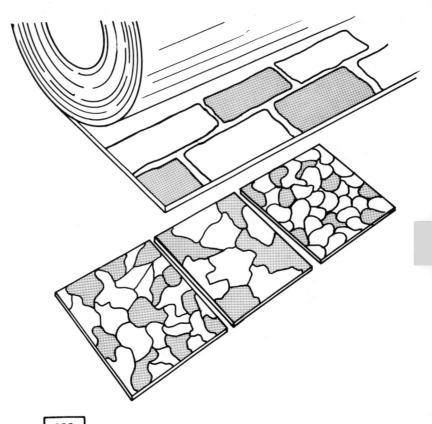

129

WALLS, FLOOR AND CEILING

Floor Coverings

Tiles are easier than sheets for the inexperienced person to install. Some models are self-adhesive, while for others the adhesive must be applied first, according to the manufacturer's directions.

- *Pure vinyl* tile is extremely durable and easy to clean, but is the most expensive of the tiles.

- *Vinyl asbestos* tile is not as comfortable underfoot as pure vinyl tile, but resists dents better and is less expensive.

- *Roto vinyl* tile is popular because of its resilience and low cost.

- *Vinyl cork* tile has the look and feel of cork, and contributes to a quiet kitchen. It is fairly expensive.

- *Rubber* tile is comfortable and durable, but is a safety hazard as it is slippery when wet.

- *Asphalt* tile is less satisfactory than the other materials, both from the standpoint of scratch-resistance and ease of cleaning.

In choosing a sheet vinyl or one of the tile floor coverings, keep in mind that light colors tend to conceal abrasions better then dark colors. Also, a textured surface will conceal abrasions better

Floor Coverings

than a smooth surface, but will also accumulate wax and dirt more quickly.

A floor covering for the kitchen that has gained popularity in recent years is carpeting. Depending on the kind of use it will get, carpeting can be very satisfactory or not. In particular, if you have a relatively quiet kitchen, predominantly used by adults or older children, carpeting will probably work out very well. Durable materials are available which are easy to install and easy to clean. These new materials do not absorb moisture or grease, and can be just wiped clean. Burn holes are easy to repair. However, young active children and pets can be hard on even the best carpeting material.

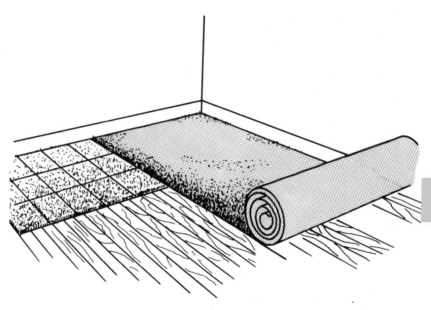

The appeal of carpeting is from its quietness and comfort. It absorbs sound and will reduce breakage of inevitably-dropped dishes. Carpeting is available in rolls or in easy-to-lay tile form.

Another material sometimes chosen for kitchen floors is wood. The best woods for this purpose are birch, beech and maple. All three have good durability, are easy to wash, and show little warping or shrinkage.

131

WALLS, FLOOR AND CEILING

Ceiling

The ceiling can be given a new coat of paint, as part of your modernization plans, or can be covered with plain or acoustical tile. A more elaborate but very effective technique is to install a suspended ceiling, particularly if you have one of the older, high-ceiling kitchens. A suspended ceiling provides a useful recess for lighting fixtures.

Wall cabinets, as mentioned earlier, should not normally extend all the way to the ceiling, because the top shelf becomes inaccessible. The space between the top of the wall cabinets and ceiling is usually filled by a soffit (also called a fascia or bulkhead). The soffit is merely an installed frontal surface, usually wood, which is then painted or wallpapered to provide an attractive finishing trim to your kitchen. In some kitchens, the soffit is covered with material to match the cabinets. Other soffits, made of translucent material, serve as recesses for light fixtures.

DECORATOR ITEMS AND ACCESSORIES

The decor or overall appearance of the kitchen is expressed in the color and pattern of counter-tops, floor, walls and ceiling, the lighting arrange-ment, and other decorator items and accessories that we have yet to consider. These include the style of cabinet doors, the door and drawer handles, chairs, curtains, etc. All of these are available in a variety of contemporary and tradi-tional designs, and their selection must remain a matter of individual taste. Window shades, for example, are now found in many bright colors, patterns and fabrics, replacing the traditional drab brown.

Some appliances, particularly dishwashers and refrigerators, have provision for a panel front which matches your cabinets. You can easily install these yourself in a few minutes.

Many accessories, built-in and otherwise, are on the market, only a few of which can be mentioned here: mixers, paper dispenser, towel racks, spice shelves, kitchen scales, can openers, char-broilers, warming drawers, infrared food warmers, instant hot water dispensers, clocks, radios, etc. Try to plan specific locations for those accessories you wish to have. Otherwise, later installation or storage may be unsatisfactory.

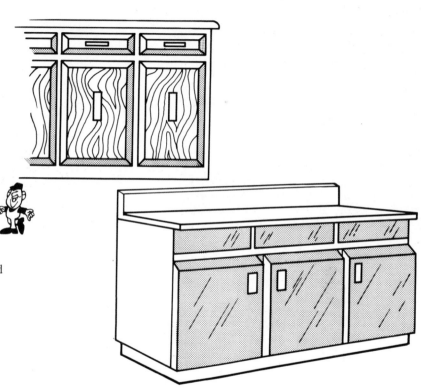

133

HOW TO PROCEED

Making Your Plan

Once you have decided to do some remodeling to your kitchen, regardless of who is going to do it or what is to be done, the first step is to get your plan down on paper. Begin by sketching your existing kitchen to scale. A good scale to use is 1/2 inch equals one foot. For example, a wall ten feet long appears as a pair of lines five inches long on your drawing.

Accurate measurement is quite important, so it is a good idea to check your measurements carefully or have somebody else check them. On the first sketch show the main structural features of your kitchen: the walls, entrances and windows. Do not show cabinets or appliances.

On a separate sheet of paper make a scale drawing of appliances and cabinets. These would be drawings of existing units and planned new units. New units can be drawn in several different sizes available, for planning purposes. Now cut out the units so they can be placed in various arrangements on your kitchen drawing.

You are now ready to experiment with different arrangements by trying different layouts of cabinets and appliances.

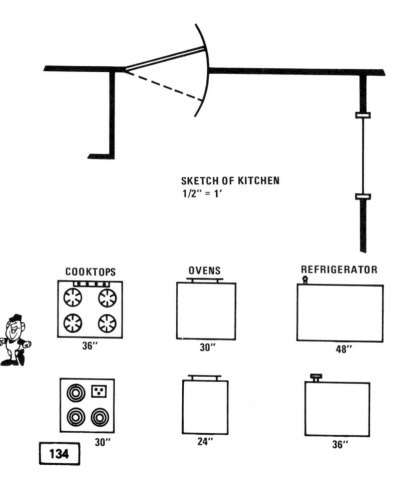

SKETCH OF KITCHEN
1/2" = 1'

COOKTOPS

36"

30"

OVENS

30"

24"

REFRIGERATOR

48"

36"

134

HOW TO PROCEED

Making Your Plan

While trying different arrangements, review the features of a good kitchen discussed earlier. See how far apart your work centers are for different configurations, and note if there is interference from traffic. Measure the space for counters and cabinets and compare with requirements which have been described. Be sure to look carefully at the location of the work and storage space, and be specific about what it will be used for. Think about details like cutlery drawers, cutting board, towel rack, etc.

In trying out different arrangements, attempt to make use of existing plumbing, vents and drains if possible. Changing the location of these items will add appreciably to the remodeling cost.

You may find that you just cannot arrive at a satisfactory arrangement. If so, consider some of the other alternatives: moving a door or window, moving or removing a wall, or adding an island or peninsula. The latter is actually the easiest, since no major structural changes are required. Base and wall cabinets for islands or peninsulas can be bought ready-made.

Be sure, in your planning, to allow enough space for any future appliance additions. If you intend to add a dishwasher later for example, leave space so you will not have to knock out cabinets and countertops.

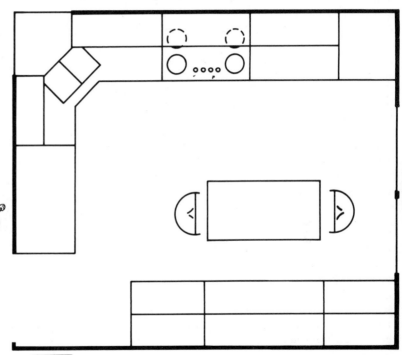

HOW TO PROCEED

Deciding What to Do Yourself

The first step is to learn what things *you* legally can do yourself. Once you have determined this, then you can decide, from among the tasks legally allowed, what you would like to attempt to do yourself.

Check with your local Department of Building and Safety to see what rules, codes and ordinances apply. These laws vary considerably from one community to another in different parts of the country. It is not necessary to check if you merely plan a new coat of paint, of course, but if you intend any structural changes, plumbing, or electrical work, investigate first. Often a licensed electrician is required for electrical work, and if you deviate, you could invalidate your home fire insurance.

When deciding what to do yourself, bear in mind that dismantling the kitchen will affect the entire family. You may find yourself eating a lot of sandwiches, washing dishes in the bathtub, etc. The amount of time that you must put up with such inconveniences will usually be less if you have expert help. The expert is also less likely to make costly mistakes, and even if he does, they are his responsibility.

If you are considering a major remodeling job, the best plan is probably a combined effort, where you do the initial preparatory work and the finishing, and you hire expert assistance for the major tasks. You can get the kitchen ready by emptying all the cabinets, removing all decorative items such as curtains, etc. If the cabinets and counter tops are to be removed, you may decide to remove them yourself. Now the professional makes any major structural changes to windows, doors or walls and does the plumbing, gas and electrical work. Whether you should install the appliances, cabinets and counter tops or have it done depends on your facility with this kind of work.

Later sections in this book describe how to do these things. Much or perhaps all of the finish work you can do yourself. This may include painting, wallpapering, paneling, or laying a new floor. If you are covering the floor in vinyl or carpet, remember that it is easier laying these materials in the tile form than in sheets.

It is essential that you obtain cost estimates before hiring expert help. This is part of the process of selecting contractors.

HOW TO PROCEED

Selecting a Contractor

If you are going to need expert assistance, you should take your plans to several contractors for bids. They may also have suggestions worth listening to. Friends may supply you with contractor's names from past experience. If not, the Yellow Pages are a good source.

Get at least two bids for the proposed work. A bid is a written description of the job including a complete list of work to be done, detailed specifications of materials, equipment manufacture and model number, and itemized costs. The bill should also specify who will obtain the necessary permit(s), if any, and who will do the preparation and cleanup work. It also must be clearly specified who will install what equipment. The prices of some ranges, dishwashers and garbage disposers include the cost of installation, and you do not want to pay for that twice.

If the two bids are close together in price, choose one of them based on your best judgment. If the bids are, say, 20% or more different, you should get a third bid to ascertain which bid is out of line.

Before making a final contractor selection, it is well to ask for references. These previous customers can tell you if they were satisfied with the contractor's work.

The final agreement, whether it be the bid form or a separate form, should include a schedule of payment, and an arbitration clause. The clause is to protect both parties in case of disagreements that may arise while the work is in progress.

HOW TO PROCEED

Sequence and Schedule

When you have selected your contractor(s), you will, with his help, establish a mutually agreeable schedule. The guiding sequence should be as follows:

- Empty all cabinets and clear surfaces
- Disconnect old appliances, including sink
- Remove cabinets and countertops
- Remove flooring and old wall tiles, paper, or paneling
- Make structural alterations in doors, windows, walls
- Repair walls where necessary
- Install subflooring
- Rough-in plumbing connections
- Install new electrical outlets and switches
- Install new appliances, cabinets and countertops
- Connect new appliances
- Remove debris and clean up
- Paint, wallpaper, install new floor
- Add decorator touches — curtains, towels, canisters, lampshades, dinette furniture, etc.

Inspections will be required after structural, plumbing and electrical work.

Not all of the above steps may apply to your remodeling job, of course. Just use the list as a guide where it applies. Also, you may want to do some of the tasks more gradually, to keep a portion of the kitchen in use for as long as possible.

REMODELING PROCEDURES

The following pages provide specific procedures for performing those kitchen modernization activities which you have decided to do yourself. Reading through the procedures may in fact help you in deciding what to attempt yourself. In any case, before starting any of the major jobs, such as REPLACING CABINETS, REPLACING COUNTERTOPS, etc., read through the procedures. You will find the following hints useful as you read:

- Each page consists of instructions accompanied by illustrations in which items are numbered. These numbers correspond to the numbers in brackets in the instructions. This allows you to easily locate and identify each item.

- The steps are arranged in numbered sequence. This sequence is logical and efficient and should be followed, except in those instances where the instructions route you out of the sequence.

- The procedures are divided into sections by major activity as shown in the contents. For example, the first section is REPLACING CABINETS. Each section is further divided if necessary, for example, Wall Cabinets, Base Cabinets.

- Where there is the possibility of personal injury or damage to equipment, a clear indication of this appears: WARNING if there is a possibility of personal injury, or CAUTION if there is a possibility of equipment damage.

Before starting the specific procedures, certain comments should be made that apply generally to all of the procedures.

1. Manufacturer's Instructions: There is a wide variety of appliances, cabinets, etc. available on the market. Specific instructions for each model cannot conceivably be provided in a book of this scope. Therefore, instructions are presented for typical installations, which which should enable you to perform the required tasks. However, it must be emphasized that you should refer to the manufacturer's instructions for your particular model. These will give you important details which cannot be included in the book.

2. Carton Contents: When you order a new appliance, fixture or cabinet, do not remove the old one until you have examined the new one carefully. If you receive a new sink in a carton, for example, open the carton, examine the sink for defects, and account for all parts. Be sure it is the

REMODELING PROCEDURES

model and size you ordered. Only when satisfied on these counts should you remove the old sink.

3. Electrical/Plumbing/Structural Changes: Follow the advice in the preceding planning sections in having contractors perform major changes in electrical wiring, plumbing, or structure of the house. All of the procedures following assume that this basic work has already been accomplished.

4. Methods of Attachment: Most cabinet installations require attachments to walls or ceilings. The attachment should be made to wall studs [2] or ceiling joists [1] where possible. These may be found by using a magnetic stud finder, by rapping on the wall, or by drilling small holes near the edge of the ceiling or near the base board.

For standard attachments to studs or joists, use number 10 wood screws [5]. Screws should be lubricated with soap or wax to make installation easier. Any bumps on the wall should be sandpapered smooth before attachment.

If the studs or joists are not in the proper position for attachment, which is often the case, alternative methods must be used. Three methods are shown here.

For wallboard or lath and plaster, use toggle bolts [3] or molly screws [6].

For a masonry surface such as brick or tile, use expanding anchors [4].

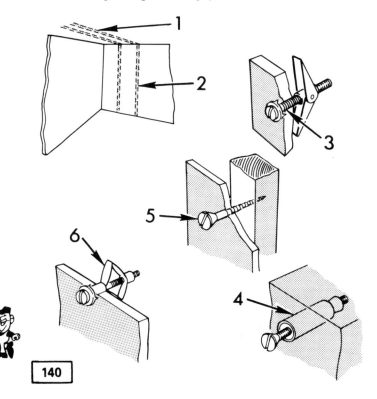

INSTALLING WALL CABINETS

Kitchen wall cabinets typically are available as individual units, with doors, shelves and essential hardware already installed.

Before starting on wall cabinet installation, be sure the following things are done:

- A detailed plan has been prepared specifying all locations and dimensions of each wall cabinet to be installed and the path of all range hood exhaust ducting.

- All obstacles have been removed from the wall cabinet work area, including the old cabinets, and the range hood, ducting and oven, if they were present before remodeling.

- Where new electrical or gas connections are needed, they have been roughed in at the appropriate locations.

Also, note these important points:

- To minimize the period of kitchen disruption, old base cabinets (other than those in the new oven area) may still be in place.

- The new oven cabinet is to be installed as part of the wall cabinet group, even though it will extend to the floor.

Wall cabinet installation requires the following tools and supplies:

Magnetic stud finder
Pencil
Spirit level
Stepladder
Power drill and 1/8-inch bit
Common screwdriver
Claw hammer
Carpenter's rule
Hand saw
Rafter square
Putty knife
Pry bar
Nails
Wood shingle
Wood strips, 1 x 2
Wood screws
Plaster corner braces

The above list excludes the cabinets and all supplies, such as mounting screws, normally furnished with the cabinets.

INSTALLING WALL CABINETS

Marking Walls

1. Mark locations of relevant studs. Draw lines plumb.

2. Check walls for flatness [3], perpendicularity [5] and corner squareness [4]. Eliminate high spots where possible.

3. Mark points on wall where shimming may be required later.

4. Check floor for flatness. Mark high point.

5. Mark top line [1] planned for wall cabinets, normally about 84 inches from high point in floor. Make line level.

6. Mark bottom line [2] planned for wall cabinets. Make line level.

7. Starting with a corner, mark walls [6] to indicate location and dimensions of each wall cabinet to be installed, including oven cabinet.

8. If range hood exhaust ducting path is to be behind soffit instead of through attic, mark wall to indicate exit point. Cut opening through wall before installing cabinets. For instructions, see Installing Range Hoods, Page 164.

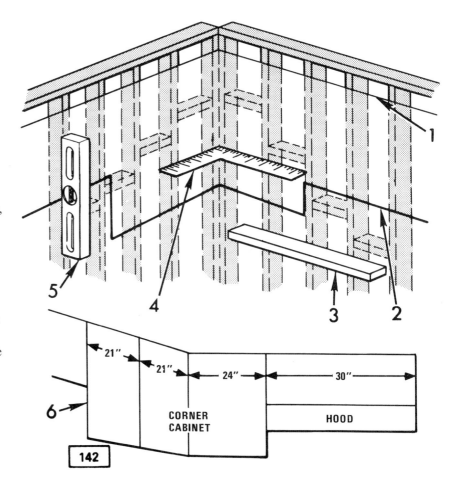

142

INSTALLING WALL CABINETS

Installing Cabinets

1. Temporarily nail cleats [1] to wall just be-
    low bottom line [2] planned for cabinets.
    Cleats will help support cabinets during
    installation.

If a corner cabinet is included, it should be
installed first.

2. Fasten first cabinet to wall with a nail
    driven only part way into studs.

3. Adjust cabinet position until plumb and
    level, using shims as necessary.

4. Firm up cabinet position with a second
    nail. Re-check plumb and level, and adjust
    as necessary.

5. Secure cabinet to wall with wood screws
    through mounting rail [4] and into studs [3].

6. Remove nails.

7. Repeat Steps 2 through 6 with remainder of
    wall cabinets.

The oven cabinet should be installed along
with the wall cabinets.

8. Remove cleats and fill all nail holes.

9. Bolt cabinets together to retain alignment.

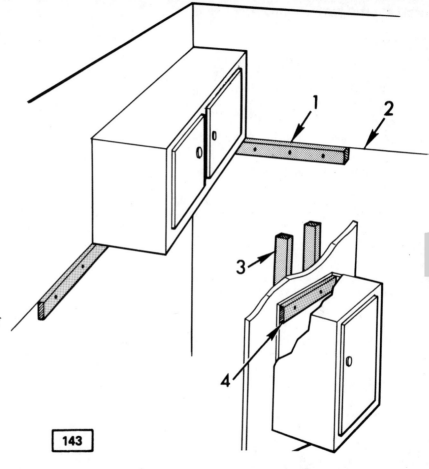

143

INSTALLING WALL CABINETS

Installing Soffit

1. Measure and cut soffit framing from 1 x 2 or 2 x 2 lumber. Construct a frame with horizontal strips [1] and vertical strips [2]. Vertical strips [2] should be spaced 16 inches apart.

2. Measure and cut paneling or drywall for outer covering [3].

3. Assemble soffit frame, using wood screws and corner braces.

If range hood exhaust ducting is to be located behind soffit, do not install soffit until ducting is in place.

4. Fasten soffit frame to ceiling joists. Set it back from cabinet front surface a distance equal to thickness of soffit paneling or drywall covering [3].

When ceiling joists are not accessible because they run in the same direction as the soffit, go up into the attic and nail some pieces of 2 x 4 between joists, along the line to be followed by the soffit.

5. Install soffit paneling or drywall covering [3].

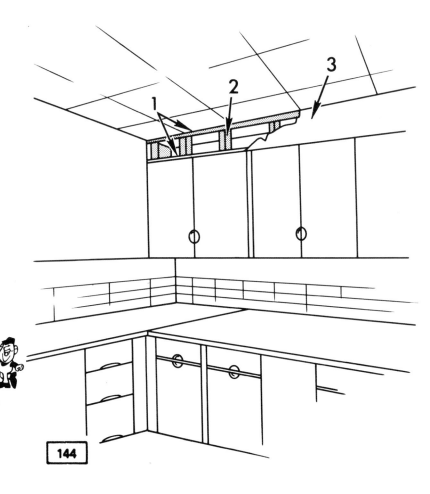

144

INSTALLING BASE CABINETS

Kitchen base cabinets typically are available as individual topless units, with doors, shelves and essential hardware already installed.

Before starting on base cabinet installation, be sure the following things are done:

- A detailed plan has been prepared specifying the location and dimensions of each base cabinet to be installed.

- All obstacles have been removed from the base cabinet work area, including the old cabinets, the sink and fittings, the dishwasher, the range, other base-level appliances, and baseboards.

- Where new electrical, gas or plumbing connections are needed, they have been roughed in at the appropriate locations.

Also, note these important points:

- The base cabinet group will include cabinet units for a sink, a dishwasher and a built-in range.

- A countertop will be installed later.

Base cabinet installation requires the following tools and supplies:

> Pencil
> Spirit level
> Power drill and 1/8-inch bit
> Common screwdriver
> Claw hammer
> Carpenter's rule
> Rafter square
> Pry bar
> Nails
> Wood shingle
> Wood screws
> Plaster

The above list excludes the cabinets and supplies, such as mounting screws, normally furnished with the cabinets.

INSTALLING BASE CABINETS

Marking Walls and Floor

1. Mark locations of relevant studs. Draw lines plumb.

2. Check walls for flatness [1] perpendicularity [3] and corner squareness [2]. Eliminate high spots where possible.

3. Mark points on wall where shimming may be required later.

4. Check floor for flatness. Mark high point.

5. Mark points on floor where shimming may be required later.

6. Starting with corner, mark walls [4] and floor [5] to indicate location and dimensions of each base cabinet to be installed.

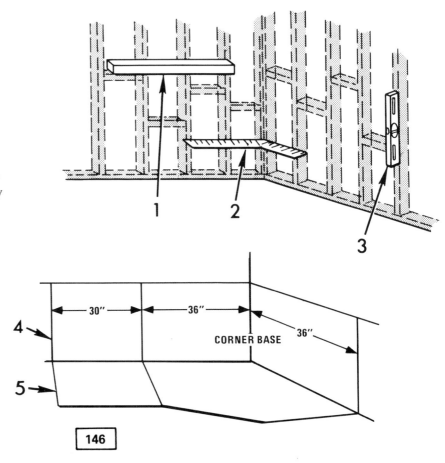

146

INSTALLING BASE CABINETS

If a corner cabinet is included, it should be installed first.

1. Move corner cabinet [3] so that front bottom edges align with reference lines on floor [1].

2. Cut four blocks of wood [2] and place at rear bottom edges of corner cabinet to hold cabinet evenly away from wall.

3. Shim corner cabinet as necessary to get it plumb and level.

4. Move other cabinets into place against wall, using floor reference lines [1] for initial positioning.

5. Shim cabinets as necessary to get them plumb, level and aligned with each other.

6. Bolt cabinets together to retain alignment.

7. Fasten cabinets to wall with wood screws into studs.

8. Re-check entire upper surface of cabinet frame to assure it is level. Remove high spots and fill in low spots, where necessary, to provide a good fit when countertop is installed later.

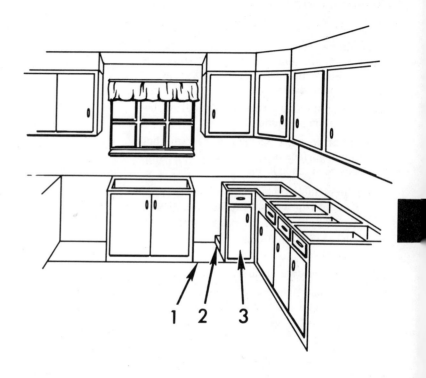

INSTALLING COUNTERTOPS

Countertops may be provided for in a number of ways. The way described here is through the use of prefabricated laminated plastic sections. The description covers six consecutive activities: selecting components, preparing sections, assembling components, installing assembly, and making sink and range cutouts.

Before starting on countertop installation, be sure the following things are done:

- All cabinets have been installed and the upper surface of the base cabinet frame has been made level.

- The countertop layout has been drawn. Countertop style and color have been selected.

- The old sink and range have been removed.

Also, note these important points:

- For illustrative purposes only, the procedure describes a U-shaped layout.

- Countertop components have not yet been ordered.

- When components arrive, they will not be pre-cut for this particular kitchen.

Countertop installation requires the following tools and supplies:

Pencil
Fine-toothed saw
Claw hammer
Tape measure
Common screwdriver
Fine-toothed file
Saw horses
Straight edge
Power drill and 1/2-inch bit
Masking tape, 1 inch wide. Use a quality masking tape such as "SCOTCH BRAND".
Transparent tape, 1 inch wide. Use a quality tape such as "SCOTCH BRAND" Magic Transparent Tape.
Nails
Wood screws

The above list excludes the countertop sections themselves and the installation kit normally obtained with the sections.

INSTALLING COUNTERTOPS

Selecting Components

1. Assume kitchen layout as indicated.

2. Note standard section shapes available: left corner (L), right corner (R) and straight (S).

3. Note standard lengths available, four feet to 12 feet, at two foot intervals.

4. Note kitchen layout calls for section shapes as follows:

   (L) Two (Sections 1 and 3)
   (R) Two (Sections 2 and 4)
   (S) None

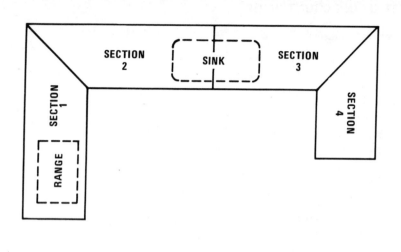

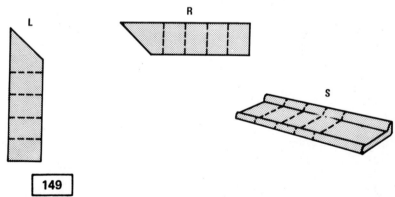

149

INSTALLING COUNTERTOPS

Selecting Components

5. Order sections as follows:
   - For Section 1 (75 inches); order 8 ft. (L)
   - For Section 2 (75 inches); order 8 ft. (R)
   - For Section 3 (66 inches); order 6 ft. (L)
   - For Section 4 (51 inches); order 6 ft. (R)

6. Order other components as follows:
   - For exposed end (A) order End Cap [1]. This component is reversible.
   - For end (B) adjoining refrigerator, order End Splash [2]. This component is reversible.

7. Note that Corner Sections are factory-mitred to fit together.

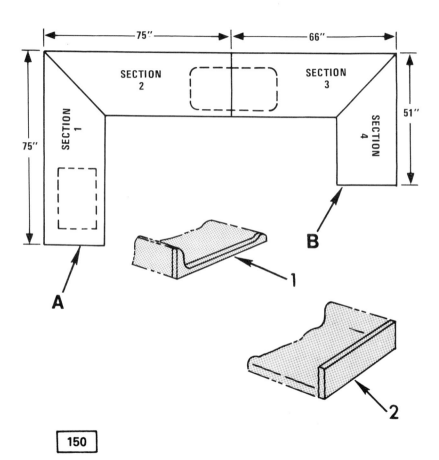

INSTALLING COUNTERTOPS

Preparing Sections

1. Label each section with a piece of masking tape.

2. On masking tape, write section number and planned length:

   Section 1   75 inches
   Section 2   75 inches
   Section 3   66 inches
   Section 4   50* inches

   * Section 4 should be 51 inches minus thickness of End Splash or 50 inches.

3. Starting at a corner tip [1], measure and mark planned length of each section. Make each marking [2] square with section edges [3].

4. Carefully double-check all measurements and markings before proceeding.

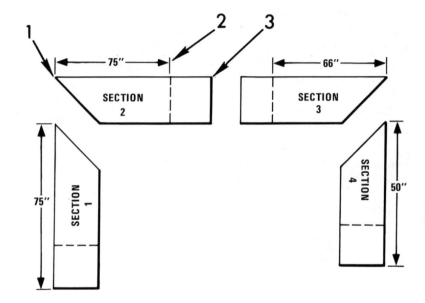

INSTALLING COUNTERTOPS

Preparing Sections

5. Place Section 1 on saw horse or work surface.

Use "SCOTCH BRAND" Magic Transparent Tape for next step to protect plastic during cutting.

6. Fasten strip of transparent tape [1] over marking [2].

7. Using a fine-toothed saw, carefully cut section to required length.

<u>CAUTION</u>

Always cut and file into finished surface to avoid damaging plastic.

8. Using a fine-toothed file, smooth cut edges as necessary.

9. Repeat Steps 5 through 8 to cut Sections 2, 3 and 4.

INSTALLING COUNTERTOPS

Assembling Components

1. Place Sections 1 and 2 together finished side down, on a soft surface.

2. Apply adhesive to mating surfaces [1].

3. Install joint fasteners in slots [2] provided. Tighten until snug but not fully tight.

4. Align front edges and top surface and tighten fasteners completely, working front to back.

5. Align backsplashes [3] and nail together.

6. Repeat Steps 1 through 5 for Sections 3 and 4.

7. Nail End Splash [4] onto Section 4.

8. Cement End Cap [5] into place on Section 1.

9. Remove excess adhesive.

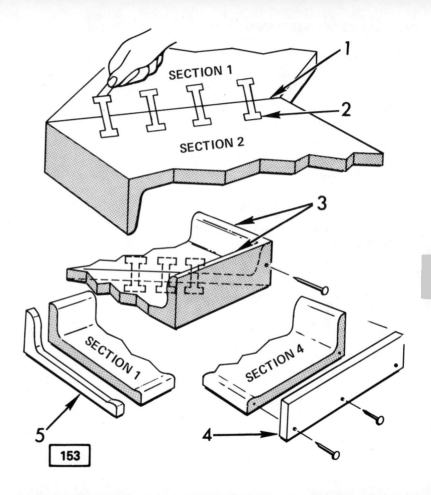

153

INSTALLING COUNTERTOPS

Installing Assembly

1. Place Sections 1 and 2 on top of cabinets, in final position.

2. Fasten Sections 1 and 2 to cabinet fixture with wood screws, from underneath.

CAUTION

Be sure the screws are not so long that they will raise or penetrate plastic surface.

3. Apply adhesive to mating surfaces of Sections 2 and 3.

4. Place Sections 3 and 4 on top of cabinets, in final position. Maintain pressure on joint between Sections 2 and 3 until adhesive dries.

5. Fasten Sections 3 and 4 to cabinet frame with wood screws, from underneath.

6. Remove excess adhesive.

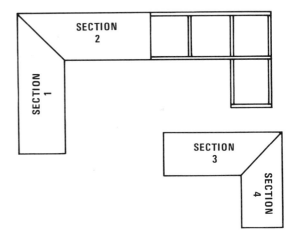

INSTALLING COUNTERTOPS

Making Sink and Range Cutouts

1. On countertop, locate center [1] of sink cabinet [2]. Make this the center of cutout required for sink.

2. Trace around sink trim ring [3] to make cutout perimeter. Align trim ring carefully before marking.

Use "SCOTCH BRAND" Magic Transparent Tape for next step to protect plastic during cutting.

3. Fasten strip of transparent tape over perimeter marking [5].

4. Bore 1/2-inch holes [4] in two opposite corners of perimeter marking.

5. Using a fine-toothed saw, cut around perimeter marking [5].

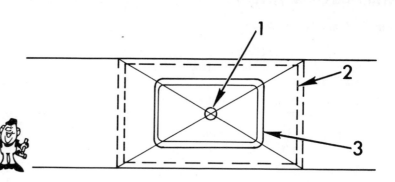

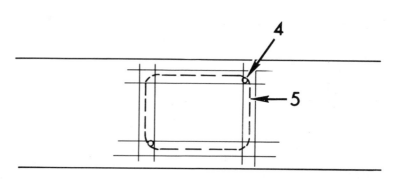

INSTALLING COUNTERTOPS

Making Sink and Range Cutouts

<u>CAUTION</u>

Always cut and file into finished surface to avoid damaging plastic.

6. Using a fine-toothed file, smooth cutout edges as necessary.

7. Repeat Steps 1 through 6 for range cutout [2], using range tub [1] as a template, directly above range cabinet.

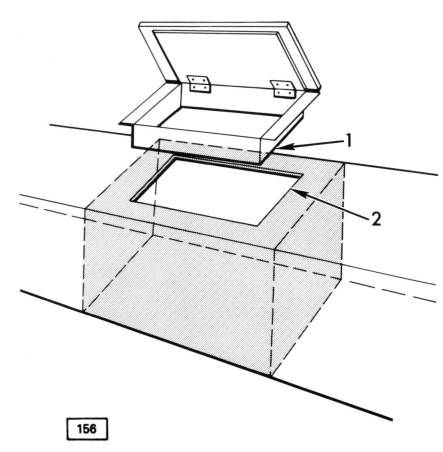

INSTALLING BUILT-IN RANGES

A typical built-in range consists of a shallow tub with a hinged top.

A cutout must be made in the countertop, to accommodate the tub.

For an electric range, electrical power must be brought to a wall beneath the counter. Normally, a power cord is carried by the range.

For a gas range, a gas supply line (with a shut-off valve) must be brought to a wall beneath the counter.

A flexible gas connector must be installed between the gas supply line and the range.

Before starting on range installation, be sure the following things are done:

- Base cabinets and countertops have been installed

- The range cutout has been made in the countertop.

- For a gas range, a gas supply line and shut-off valve have been brought to a wall beneath the counter.

- For an electric range, electrical power has been brought to a wall outlet beneath the counter.

Range installation requires the following tools and supplies:

> Common screwdriver*
> Phillips screwdriver*
> Adjustable wrench*
> Pipe wrench*
> Flexible connector.* Flexible connectors are corrugated lines which are made so that they can be easily bent. They allow easier hookup between appliances and gas supply lines. They are available in different lengths.
> Soap suds*

*For gas range only

The above list excludes tools and supplies required to install the electrical supply circuit and gas supply line. It also excludes the range itself and components normally furnished with it.

INSTALLING BUILT-IN RANGES

WARNING

Turn off power at circuit breaker box, OR be sure gas is turned off at meter outside house.

1. On gas range, attach flexible connector [4] to tub[1].

2. Lower gas or electric range through counter-top cutout [2], flexible connector [4] or power cord [7] first.

3. Adjust range position until it appears even in all directions.

4. Fasten tub [1] to countertop with wood screws [3].

5. Connect power line [6] to power source, OR attach flexible connector [4] to gas shut-off valve [5].

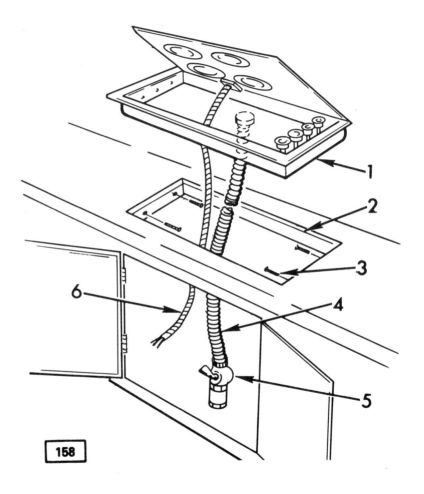

158

INSTALLING BUILT-IN RANGES

6. Turn on power and verify electric range operation through range top controls.

    ### OR

    Turn gas range top controls to OFF position. Turn shut-off valve [1] to open position.

7. Check for gas leaks by applying soap suds to each connection. Bubbles should form at points of leakage.

8. Correct all gas leaks, and recheck before putting range into operation.

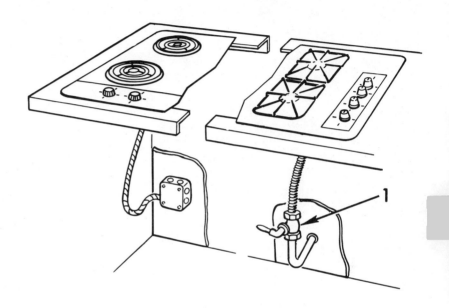

INSTALLING BUILT-IN OVENS

In a typical oven installation, the oven is mounted in a backless cabinet above floor level.

The oven requires a level support base strong enough to sustain 100-130 pounds. Such support is usually built into the oven cabinet.

Electrical and gas connection points are in back. Mounting provisions are in front.

For a gas oven, a gas supply line (with a shut-off valve) must be brought to a wall beneath the oven.

A flexible gas connector must be installed between the gas supply line and the oven.

During installation, the gas connector is attached to the oven from the inside of the oven.

For an electric oven, a separate electrical circuit must be provided to serve the heating unit. The oven carries its own power cord.

For a gas oven or a microwave oven, electrical power (normal house current) must be brought to a wall behind the oven. Each oven carries its own power cord.

Before starting an oven installation, be sure the following things are done:

- An oven cabinet has been installed, providing a level support base strong enough to hold the oven.

- For a gas oven, a gas supply line and shut-off valve have been brought to a wall behind and beneath the oven cabinet.

- For all types of ovens, electrical power has been brought to a wall outlet behind the oven cabinet.

- For an electric oven, a separate electrical circuit has been installed.

Oven installation requires the following tools and supplies:

Common screwdriver
Phillips screwdriver
Adjustable wrench*
Pipe wrench*
Pipe compound*
Flexible connector*
Soap suds*

*For gas oven only

The above list excludes tools and supplies required to install electrical circuits and gas supply lines. It also excludes the oven itself and components normally furnished with it.

Go to Page 161 to begin installing a gas oven. For electric or microwave ovens, go to Page 163.

INSTALLING BUILT-IN OVENS

Gas Oven

WARNING

Be sure gas shut-off valve [3] is in CLOSED position.

1. Remove doors and racks from oven.

2. Remove cover plate [4] from rear wall of oven.

3. Attach flexible connector [2] to gas shut-off valve [3]. Position end of connector [2] so that it is accessible from cover plate opening [4].

4. Plug power cord [1] into wall outlet.

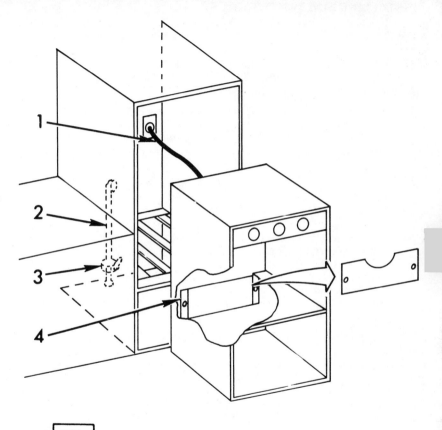

INSTALLING BUILT-IN OVENS

Gas Oven

5. Slide oven into cabinet. Be sure it is level.

6. Attach flexible connector [2] to gas fitting on oven.

7. Turn oven controls to OFF position. Turn shut-off valve [3] to OPEN position.

8. Check for leaks by applying soap suds to each connection. Bubbles should form at gas leaks.

9. Correct all gas leaks and recheck connections before proceeding further.

10. Install cover plate over opening [1].

11. Check that all oven controls work properly.

12. Fasten oven to cabinet as required.

13. Install oven doors and racks.

14. Install oven trim.

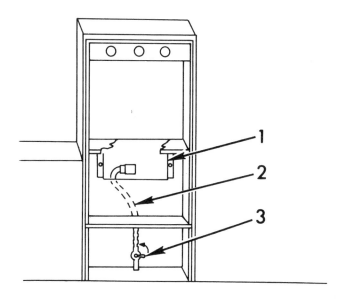

INSTALLING BUILT-IN OVENS

Electric Oven/Microwave Oven

1. Slide oven part way into oven cabinet.
    Connect power line to power source.

2. Slide oven remainder of way into cabinet.
    Be sure it is level.

3. Verify oven operation through oven
    controls [1].

4. Fasten oven to cabinet frame with attach-
    ments provided.

5. Install oven trim [2].

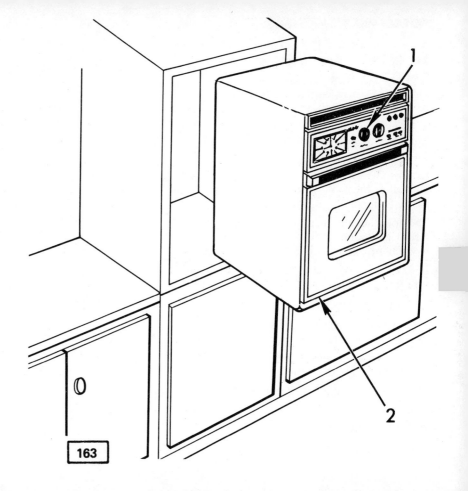

163

INSTALLING RANGE HOODS

A typical range hood layout consists of a hood with built-in exhaust fan and light, and associated exhaust ducting.

The hood is surface-mounted to the cabinet above the range.

Openings must be cut in cabinet shelves, ceiling and (sometimes) roof, to accommodate the exhaust ducting.

Exhaust ducting must extend through an exterior wall or the roof. Ducts must be capped to prevent backdraft.

The hood fan and light are served by a built-in electrical junction box. Electrical power must be brought to that point.

Before starting on range hood installation, be sure the following things are done:

- Wall cabinets have been installed.

- An exhaust duct path has been planned leading through an exterior wall.

- Electrical power has been brought to the point of hood junction box, in a conduit.

Also, note these important points:

- Shelf cutouts have not yet been made for the hood exhaust ducting.

- Where the planned exhaust ducting path is directly behind a soffit, the soffit has not yet been installed.

Range hood installation requires the following tools and supplies:

> Pencil
> Power drill and 3/4-inch bit
> Keyhole saw
> Common screwdriver
> Extension light

The above list excludes tools and supplies required to install the electrical supply circuit. It also excludes the ducting, the range hood, and components normally furnished with them.

INSTALLING RANGE HOODS

Hood installation is best performed by two people.

1. Hold hood in position above range. Note exact location of hood collar [3]. Mark cabinet shelves [2] above hood to show location and shape of path for duct leading from collar.

2. Cut openings [1] in cabinet shelves, large enough for passage of duct and electrical conduit.

3. If duct is to go through attic, cut opening in ceiling similar to those in shelves. If duct is not to go through attic, cut ceiling opening large enough for electrical conduit only.

WARNING
Turn off power at fuse or circuit breaker box.

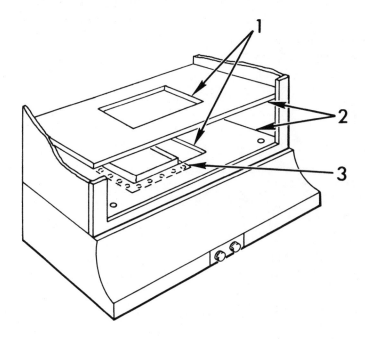

INSTALLING RANGE HOODS

4. Bring electrical conduit [1] to junction box [3] in hood.

5. Fasten hood to cabinet. Connect conduit [1] to junction box [3].

6. Connect electrical wires in junction box. Be sure to join white wires to white wires and black wires to black wires.

7. Turn on electrical power.

8. Check operation of hood fan and light.

9. Install duct [2] through shelf openings. Attach duct [2] to collar [4] on hood.

If fumes are to be vented through an exterior wall of house, go to Step 10 to install remainder of ducts.

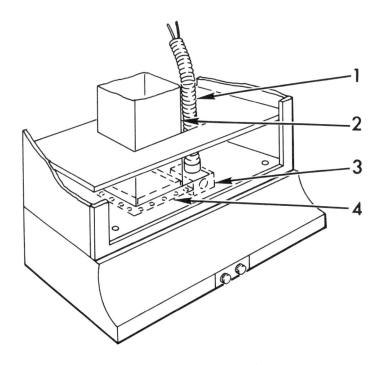

INSTALLING RANGE HOODS

10. On inner surface of wall, trace shape of required opening [2], using a ducting segment [1] as a template.

11. Cut opening [3] through inner wall large enough for passage of ducting.

12. When outer wall is accessible through inner wall opening, locate center [4] in inner surface of outer wall.

13. Bore small hole through center [4] from inside. If exterior is stone, brick, or stucco, use masonry drill.

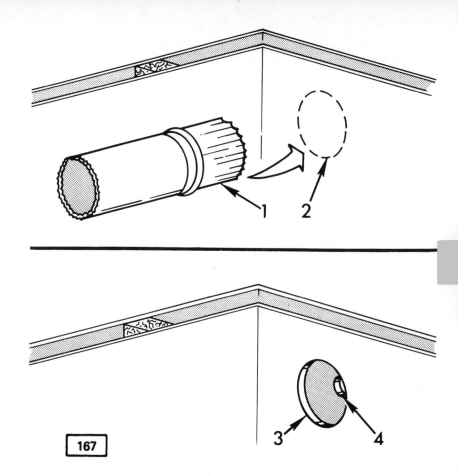

167

INSTALLING RANGE HOODS

14. Complete cutting of outer wall opening [2] from outside house, using center hole as a guide.

15. Insert exterior duct cap [1] through opening in wall, and connect it to final segment of ducting [3] inside.

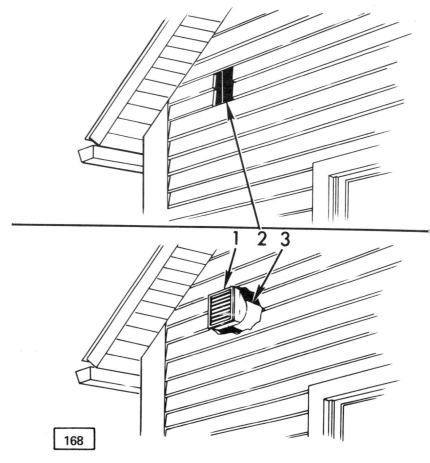

168

REPLACING SINKS

Sink replacement is described in terms of six consecutive activities: removing sinks, removing fittings, installing shut-off valves, installing fittings, installing sinks, and connecting sinks.

The procedure covers tiled-over sinks and sinks mounted by means of a trim ring.

Before starting on sink replacement, be sure the following things have been done:

- Base cabinets and countertops have been installed.

- The sink cutout has been made in the countertop.

- All required plumbing connections have been roughed in at the intended sink locations.

Also, note these important points:

- For illustrative purposes only, the removal procedure describes a dual-compartment sink without a garbage disposal or dishwasher. The installation procedure describes a dual-compartment sink with provisions for a garbage disposer, and a dishwasher.

- The garbage disposer has a built-in dishwasher inlet.

- If shut-off valves are lacking in the old set-up, plan to install them. Page 173.

- Plan to replace the water supply lines while installing the shut-off valves.

Sink replacement requires the following tools and supplies:

> Adjustable wrench
> Pipe wrench
> Common screwdriver
> Pliers
> Ballpeen hammer
> Cold chisel
> Basin wrench
> Hack saw
> Putty knife
> Shallow pan
> Plumbers putty
> Pipe compound
> Shut-off valve
> Dual-outlet shut-off valve
> Two flexible connectors
> End outlet
> Tile adhesive
> Tile grout

The above list excludes tools and supplies required to relocate waste line or water source lines. It also excludes the sink itself and fittings and components normally obtained with the sink.

REPLACING SINKS

Removing Sink

1. Turn off water and drain both lines into shallow pan.

2. Remove trap [2] by loosening slip joint nuts[1]. Empty water into pan.

3. Disconnect water supply lines [5] from faucet shanks [3] by loosening coupling nuts[4] with basin wrench.

If the sink is supported by a wall hanger, go to Step 7.

If edges of sink are tiled over at the countertop, go to Step 4.

If the sink is joined to the countertop with a metal trim ring, go to Step 6.

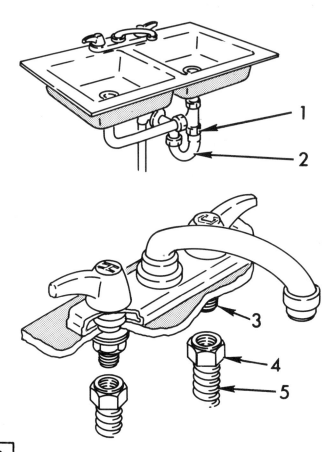

REPLACING SINKS

Removing Sink

4. Using ballpeen hammer and sharp cold chisel, remove enough tiles [4] to expose edges of sink.

CAUTION

Handle tiles carefully to avoid damage or loss.

5. Remove grout and adhesive from exposed countertop surface and from all tiles which are to be saved for re-use. Go to Step 7.

6. Loosen setscrews [3] from trim ring [1] and remove lugs [5]. The sink will remain supported on countertop during this step.

7. Lift sink out of countertop or away from wall, with fittings still attached.

CROSS SECTION OF TRIM RING

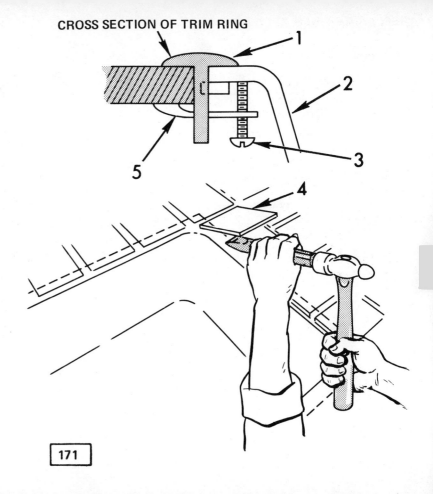

REPLACING SINKS

Removing Fittings

1. Remove locknuts [5] from each faucet shank [4]. Lift out faucet.

2. Remove locknut [7] from each tail piece [8]. Lift out strainers [6].

3. Bend trim ring tabs [3] away from sink flange [2]. Lift off trim ring [1].

4. Remove old putty from all fittings to be re-used.

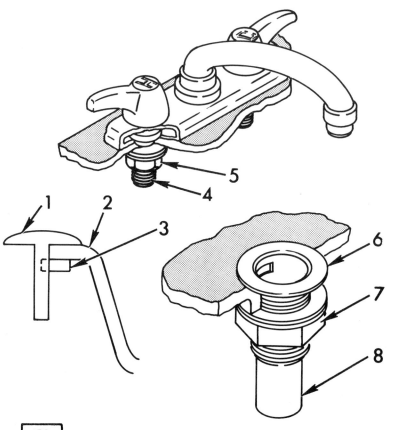

REPLACING SINKS

Installing Shut-Off Valves

Each water line requires its own shut-off valve [4, 5].

The shut-off valve [5] on the hot water line should have two outlets [7], so that it may serve the dishwasher as well as the sink.

1. Disconnect the water lines [1] from hot and cold source pipes in such a way as to leave male threads [2] exposed.

2. On cold water line, attach a single-outlet shut-off valve [4]. Use pipe compound on male threads.

3. On hot water line, attach a dual-outlet shut-off valve [5]. Use pipe compound on male threads.

4. Attach flexible connectors [3] to valve outlets facing sink.

5. Attach caps [6] to valve outlet [7] facing dishwasher.

6. Turn shut-off valves to CLOSED position.

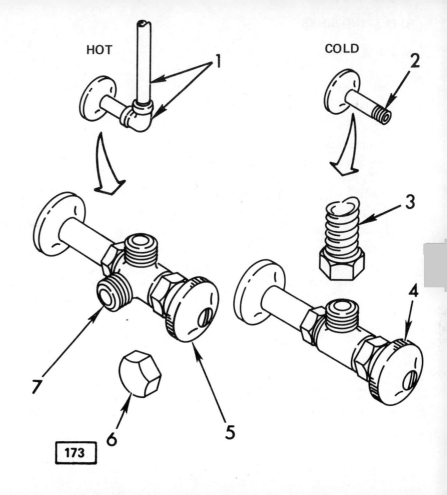

173

REPLACING SINKS

Installing Fittings

1. Apply plumbers putty around topside of faucet openings [7].

2. Insert faucet shanks through openings [7].

3. Install washers [6] and locknuts [5].

4. Tighten locknuts [5]. Remove excess putty.

5. Apply plumbers putty around topside of spray hose opening [2].

6. Insert spray hose shank [1] through opening [2].

7. Install locknut [3].

8. Tighten locknut [3]. Remove excess putty.

9. Attach spray hose to spray hose shank [1] and faucet center [4].

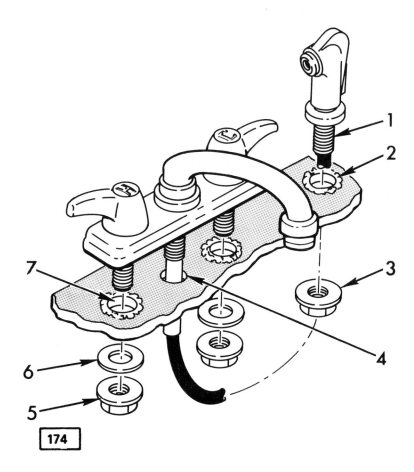

174

REPLACING SINKS

Installing Fittings

10. Apply plumbers putty around topside of drain opening [3] not to be used for garbage disposer.

Garbage disposer fittings will be installed later.

11. Insert strainer [1] through opening [3].

12. Install washer [4] and locknut [5] on tailpiece [2].

13. Tighten locknut [5]. Remove excess putty.

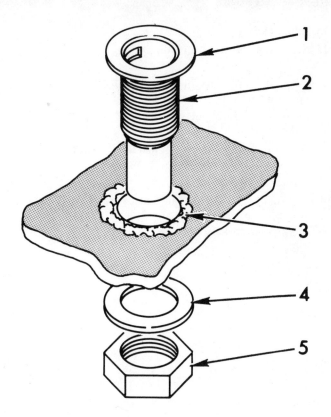

REPLACING SINKS

Installing Sink

If sink is to be mounted in a tiled countertop, go to Step 1.

If sink is to be mounted in a countertop by means of a trim ring, go to Page 177, Step 6.

1. Apply plumbers putty to underside of sink flange [1].

2. Mount sink in cutout [2], making it even in all directions.

3. Remove excess putty.

4. Cement tiles [3] back into place around sink perimeter.

5. Apply grout between new tiles [3].

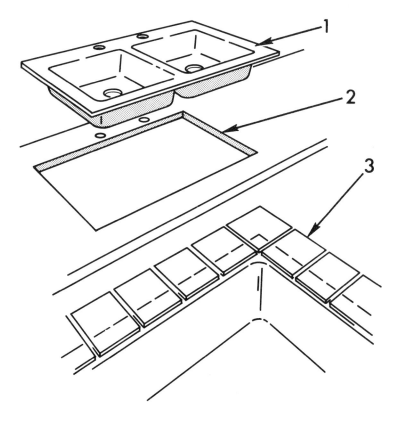

REPLACING SINKS

Installing Sink

6. Apply plumbers putty to underside of trim ring [1].

7. Place trim ring [1] on sink flange [2]. Secure by bending tabs [3] inward.

8. Lower sink [2] and trim ring [1] into countertop opening and adjust until even.

9. Insert lugs [5] through trim ring slots [4].

10. Secure sink to countertop by tightening setscrews [6].

11. Remove excess putty.

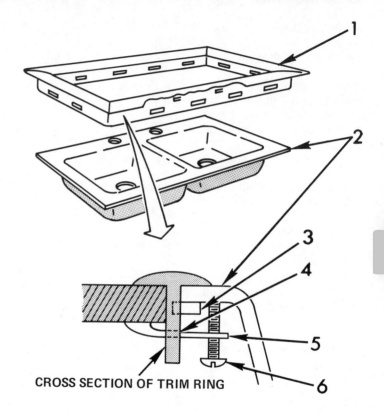

CROSS SECTION OF TRIM RING

REPLACING SINKS

Connecting Sink

Sink fittings must be installed. Page 174.

The water supply lines (in the form of flexible connectors) and shut-off valves, are already connected to the source pipes as the result of Installing Shut-off Valves, Page 173.

CAUTION

Handle flexible connectors carefully to prevent cracking them.

1. Gently shape flexible connectors (3) until they align squarely with faucet shanks (1).

2. Attach flexible connectors [3] to faucet shanks [1]. Tighten coupling nuts [2] with basin wrench.

Before proceeding to Step 3, complete Installing Garbage Disposer, Page 180.

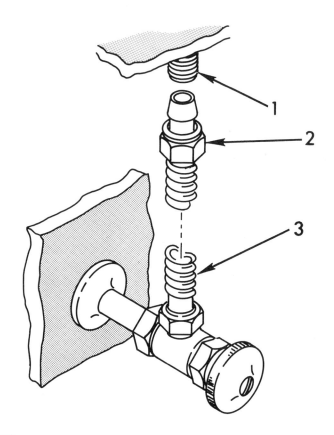

REPLACING SINKS

Connecting Sink

3. Loosely connect end outlet [5] to garbage disposer discharge tube [1] and tailpiece [3] of other drain.

4. Loosely connect trap [6] to waste line [2] and end outlet [5].

5. Adjust components [5] and [6] until properly aligned.

6. Tighten all slip joint nuts [4].

7. Turn on water and check for leaks.

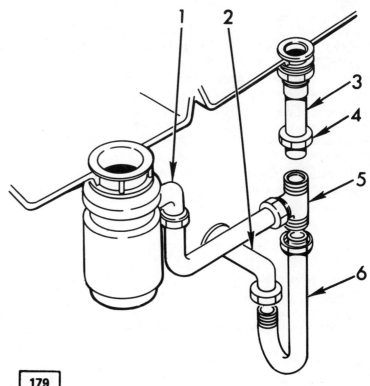

179

INSTALLING GARBAGE DISPOSERS

A typical garbage disposer is supported beneath the sink drain by means of a sink-mounting assembly.

Electrical power must be brought to a wall beneath the sink, via a circuit controlled by a wall switch near the sink. Normally, a power cord is carried by the disposer.

The disposer carries a discharge tube that connects to the existing waste line.

Disposer height must be compatible with the vertical clearance below the sink. Specifically, the discharge tube must end at a point higher than the center of the waste pipe.

Before starting on garbage disposer installation, be sure the following things are done:

- The sink has been installed.

- The water lines have been connected.

- Shut-off valves are in CLOSED position.

- Adequate vertical clearance has been found to exist for disposer.

- Electrical power has been brought to a wall outlet in the sink cabinet, through a a switch six feet away from the sink center-line.

Garbage disposer installation requires the following tools and supplies:

> Common screwdriver
> Putty knife
> Adjustable wrench

The above list excludes tools and supplies required to install the electrical supply circuit. It also excludes the garbage disposer itself and the components normally furnished with it.

INSTALLING GARBAGE DISPOSERS

1. Apply plumbers putty around topside of drain opening [2] to be used for garbage disposer.

2. Insert sink sleeve [1] through drain opening.

3. From underneath sink, attach disposer mounting assembly [4] and secure with snap ring [3].

4. Tighten mounting screws [5] evenly and remove excess putty.

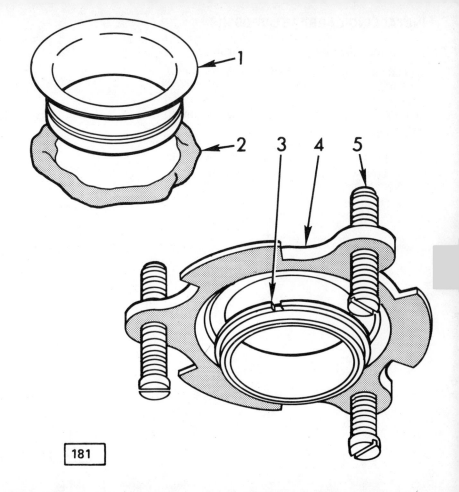

181

INSTALLING GARBAGE DISPOSERS

5. Install discharge tube [1] on disposer.

6. Raise disposer [4] into mounting assembly [2] by turning collar [3].

Before proceeding to Step 7, complete Connecting Sink, Page 178.

7. Plug power cord into wall outlet. Use wall switch to verify disposer operation.

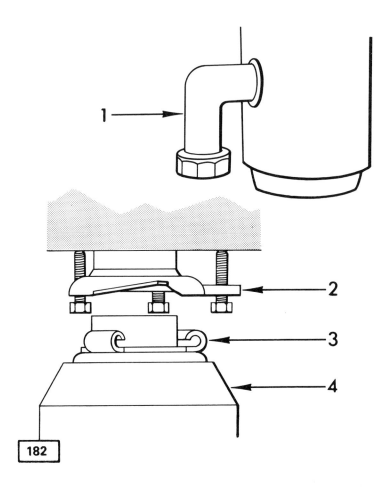

182

INSTALLING BUILT-IN DISHWASHERS

A typical built-in dishwasher is mounted in a cabinet at floor level.

Electrical and plumbing connection points are on one side, near the front. Mounting provisions are in front. Leveling is required.

A flexible connector (usually copper tubing) must be installed between the hot water supply line and the dishwasher. The line must be equipped with a shut-off valve.

The dishwasher discharge hose must be connected to the existing sink drain or garbage disposer.

A separate electrical circuit must be provided to serve the dishwasher heating unit.

Before starting on dishwasher installation, be sure the following things are done:

- Base cabinets and countertops have been installed.

- Electrical power has been brought to the point of the dishwasher junction box, in a conduit.

- A dual-outlet shut-off valve has been installed in the hot water supply line.

Also, note these important points:

- The sink has been installed and connected, adjacent to the dishwasher.

- A garbage disposer has been installed with a built-in dishwasher inlet.

- The sink is equipped with an air gap attachment.

Dishwasher installation requires the following tools and supplies:

> Common screwdriver
> Phillips screwdriver
> Adjustable wrench
> Power drill and 1-inch bit
> Tube bender
> Tube cutter
> Compression fitting elbow
> Copper tubing, type L

The above list excludes tools and supplies required to install electrical circuits. It also excludes the dishwasher itself and components normally furnished with it.

INSTALLING BUILT-IN DISHWASHERS

1. Be sure hot water dual-outlet shut-off valve [4] is in CLOSED position.

2. Remove cap [5] from shut-off valve outlet facing dishwasher.

3. Determine path to be followed by new hot water line [6], from shut-off valve [4] to washer. Mark point where opening [7] will be needed in sink cabinet wall.

CAUTION

Handle tubing carefully to prevent cracking.

4. Using tube bender, shape copper tubing to follow planned path.

5. Using tubing cutter, cut tubing squarely at each end.

6. Determine path to be followed by discharge hose [2] from washer to air gap attachment [1] to disposer [3]. Note that opening [7] will have to be large enough for water line and discharge hose.

7. Cut opening [7] in wall.

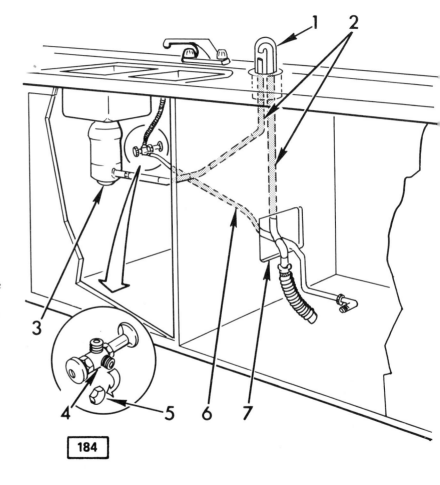

184

INSTALLING BUILT-IN DISHWASHERS

WARNING

Turn off power at fuse or circuit breaker box.

8. Bring electrical conduit [7] to point where dishwasher junction box [6] will be after dishwasher installation.

9. Connect compression elbow [8] to dishwasher.

10. Slide dishwasher part way into dishwasher cabinet. Remove front base cover [9].

11. Connect house leads in conduit [7] to dishwasher leads in junction box [6].

12. Route discharge hose [1] through wall opening [2] and connect to dishwasher with hose clamp [4].

13. Route water line [3] through wall opening [2] and connect to compression elbow [8]. Tighten compression nut [5].

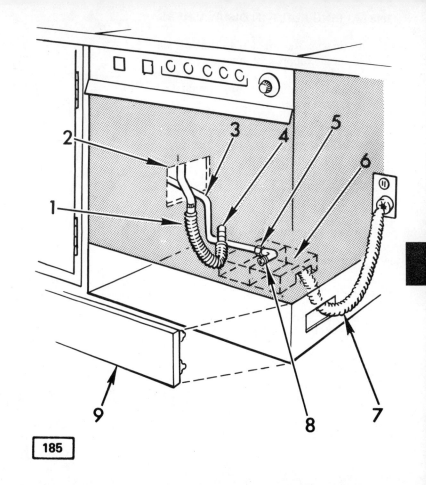

INSTALLING BUILT-IN DISHWASHERS

14. Connect water line [2] to shut-off valve [1]. Tighten compression nut.

15. Remove plug from dishwasher inlet of garbage disposer.

16. Connect dishwasher discharge hose [3] to dishwasher inlet, using coupling [4].

17. Slide dishwasher remainder of way in and adjust until level, using shims as necessary.

18. Fasten dishwasher to cabinet frame with attachments provided.

19. Turn on water.

20. Turn on power.

21. Start dishwasher. Check for leaks and verify dishwasher operation.

22. Reinstall front base cover.

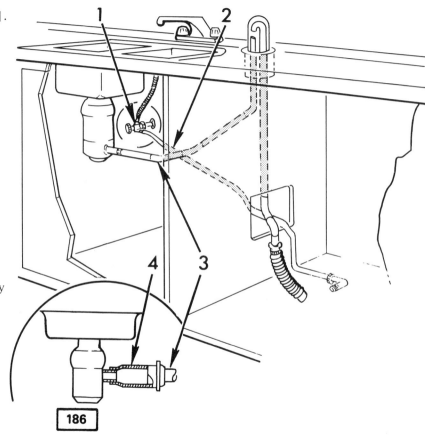

186